First Workshop on Multilingual Modeling 2012

AA004704

(MM 2012)

Jeju Island, Korea
13 July 2012

ISBN: 978-1-62276-600-0

Printed from e-media with permission by:

Curran Associates, Inc.
57 Morehouse Lane
Red Hook, NY 12571

CURRAN ASSOCIATES INC. proceedings.com

Some format issues inherent in the e-media version may also appear in this print version.

Printed by Curran Associates, Inc. (2012)

For permission requests, please contact the Association for Computational Linguistics at the address below.

Association for Computational Linguistics
209 N. Eighth Street
Stroudsburg, Pennsylvania 18360

Phone: 1-570-476-8006
Fax: 1-570-476-0860

acl@aclweb.org

Additional copies of this publication are available from:

Curran Associates, Inc.
57 Morehouse Lane
Red Hook, NY 12571 USA
Phone: 845-758-0400
Fax: 845-758-2634
Email: curran@proceedings.com
Web: www.proceedings.com

Introduction

The burgeoning community of multilingual users poses variety of new problems and also enables new opportunities. The large number of multilingual corpora requires effective and scalable ways for organizing them. This additional data in different languages provides a different perspective. Resource poor languages can utilize the training data available in other languages and improve the accuracies of monolingual applications.

Recently, we have seen an increasing number of researchers working on multilingual problems varying from mining comparable corpora from the web to multilingual part-of-speech tagging. It is encouraging to see how the abundant training data in a resource rich languages (such as English) is used along with very little training data in the target language to solve problems in resource-poor languages. In addition, resource rich languages have been used successfully to bridge the language barrier between two resource poor languages. This workshop is aimed to bring researchers working on different aspects of multilingualism to a common ground to share their experiences so that the entire community can benefit.

We received a total of 13 submissions. After a rigorous review process we selected 4 papers for presentation at the workshop. We would like to thank the members of the Program Committee for their excellent work — the reviews were all very thorough, carefully written, and detailed, and helped the authors to improve their papers.

This workshop features a mix of equal number of Invited Talks (IT), Invited Papers (IP) and Contribution Talks (CT). We are experimenting with this format to improve the quality of the discussions among the participants. We spent a considerable amount of time in selecting the IPs. These are by invitation only and are not be included in the workshop proceedings.

Organizers:

Jagadeesh Jagarlamudi (University of Maryland, USA)
Sujith Ravi (Google, USA)
Xiaojun Wan (Peking University, China)
Hal Daumé III (University of Maryland, USA)

Program Committee:

Kumaran A (Microsoft Research, India)
Pushpak Bhattacharyya (Indian Institute of Technology, India)
Srinivas Bangalore (AT&T Labs-Research, USA)
Hal Daumé III (University of Maryland, USA)
Kareen Darwish (Qatar Computing Research Institute, Qatar)
Dipanjan Das (Carnegie Mellon University, USA)
Marcello Federico (FBK – Fondazione Bruno Kessler, Tirento, Italy)
Anna Feldman (Montclair State University, USA)
Wei Gao (Qatar Computing Research Institute, Qatar)
Jagadeesh Jagarlamudi (University of Maryland, USA)
Heng Ji (City University of New York)
Mitesh Khapra (Indian Institute of Technology, India)
Alexandre Klementiev (Saarland University, USA)
Kevin Knight (USC/ISI, USA)
Yang Liu (Tsinghua University, China)
Paul McNamee (Johns Hopkins University, USA)
Rada Mihalcea (University of North Texas, USA)
Xiaochuan Ni (Microsoft)
Doug Oard (University of Maryland, USA)
Reinhard Rapp (Johannes Gutenberg-Universität Mainz, Germany)
Ari Rappoport (The Hebrew University, Israel)
Sujith Ravi (Google, USA)
Benjamin Snyder (University of Wisconsin-Madison, USA)
Benno Stein (Bauhaus-Universität Weimar, Germany)
Sebastian Stüker (Karlsruhe Institute of Technology, Germany)
Jun'ichi Tsujii (Microsoft Research Asia)
Kentaro Torisawa (NICT, Japan)
Raghavendra Udupa (Microsoft Research, India)
Xiaojun Wan (Peking University, China)
Mausam (University of Washington, USA)

Invited Speakers:

Slav Petrov, Google
Reinhard Rapp, University of Leeds
Benjamin Snyder, University of Wisconsin-Madison

Table of Contents

Workshop Program

Friday, July 13, 2012

9:00	Invited Talk by Reinhard Rapp Bilingual Lexicon Extraction Using Parallel and Comparable Corpora
9:40	*Implementing a Language-Independent MT Methodology* Sokratis Sofianopoulos, Marina Vassiliou and George Tambouratzis
10:05	Bilingual Lexicon Extraction from Comparable Corpora Using Label Propagation Akihiro Tamura, Taro Watanabe and Eiichiro Sumita (Invited Paper)
10:30	Coffee break
11:00	Invited Talk by Benjamin Snyder Multilingual Modeling: Current Work and Future Frontiers
11:40	*The Study of Effect of Length in Morphological Segmentation of Agglutinative Languages* Loganathan Ramasamy, Zdeněk Žabokrtský and Sowmya Vajjala
12:05	Unsupervised Structure Prediction with Non-Parallel Multilingual Guidance Shay B. Cohen, Dipanjan Das and Noah A. Smith (Invited Paper)
12:30	Lunch break
2:00	Invited Talk by Slav Petrov Multilingual Syntactic Analysis
2:40	*Language Independent Named Entity Identification using Wikipedia* Mahathi Bhagavatula, Santosh GSK and Vasudeva Varma
3:05	Cross-Lingual Parse Disambiguation based on Semantic Correspondence Lea Frermann and Francis Bond (Invited Paper)
3:30	Coffee break
4:00	Learning Discriminative Projections for Text Similarity Measures Wen-tau Yih, Kristina Toutanova, John Platt, and Chris Meek (Invited Paper)
4:25	Untangling the Cross-Lingual Link Structure of Wikipedia Gerard de Melo and Gerhard Weikum (Invited Paper)

Friday, July 13, 2012 (continued)

4:50 *A Comparable Corpus Based on Aligned Multilingual Ontologies*
Roger Granada, Lucelene Lopes, Carlos Ramisch, Cassia Trojahn, Renata Vieira and Aline Villavicencio

5:15 Discussion

Implementing a language-independent MT methodology

Sokratis Sofianopoulos
ILSP / Athena R.C.
Artemidos 6 & Epidavrou
Athens, Greece
s_sofian @ilsp.gr

Marina Vassiliou
ILSP / Athena R.C.
Artemidos 6 & Epidavrou
Athens, Greece
mvas@ilsp.gr

George Tambouratzis
ILSP / Athena R.C.
Artemidos 6 & Epidavrou
Athens, Greece
giorg_t@ilsp.gr

Abstract

The current paper presents a language-independent methodology, which facilitates the creation of machine translation (MT) systems for various language pairs. This methodology is implemented in the PRESEMT hybrid MT system. PRESEMT has the lowest possible requirements on specialised resources and tools, given that for many languages (especially less widely used ones) only limited linguistic resources are available. In PRESEMT, the main translation process comprises two phases. The first one, **Structure selection**, determines the overall structure of a target language (TL) sentence, drawing on syntactic information from a small bilingual corpus. The second phase, **Translation equivalent selection**, relies on models extracted solely from monolingual corpora to implement translation disambiguation, determine intra-phrase word order and handle functional words. This paper proposes extracting information for disambiguation from the monolingual corpus. Experimental results indicate that such information substantially contributes in improving translation quality.

1 Introduction

Currently most language-independent MT approaches are based on the statistical machine translation (SMT) paradigm (Koehn, 2010). SMT has proved to be particularly amenable to new language pairs, provided the necessary training data are available. The main SMT constraint is the need for SL-TL bilingual corpora of a sufficient size (at least several hundreds of thousands of sentences) to allow the building of accurate translation models. Such corpora are hard to find, particularly for less widely used languages. Furthermore, SMT translation accuracy largely depends on the quality of the bilingual corpora as well as their relevance to the domain of text to be translated. For instance, parliament proceedings (among the most widely available corpora) may not suffice to train MT systems aimed towards technical manuals or news articles.

Example-Based Machine Translation (EBMT) is another MT paradigm, where a set of SL sentences are provided together with their TL reference translations. Translations are generated by analogy, where for an input sentence the most similar SL side from the sentence set is determined and the corresponding TL side sentence is used to generate the translation. Hybrid MT systems combining EBMT and SMT techniques have been proposed (cf. Groves & Way, 2005 and Phillips, 2011).

As an alternative to SMT, techniques for creating MT systems using more limited but easily obtainable resources have been proposed. Even if these methods do not achieve an accuracy as high as that of SMT, their ability to develop MT systems with very limited resources confers to them an important advantage. The present article focusses on the development of such a methodology.

2 MT systems utilising low-cost resources

A number of methods for the automatic inference of templates for the structural transfer from SL to TL have been proposed. Notably, Caseli et al. (2008) have proposed generating resources such as bilingual transfer rules and, more importantly, shallow transfer rules from parallel corpora. In a related set-up, Sanchez-Martinez et al. (2009) suggest using small parallel corpora only to extract transfer rules, assuming that a sufficient bilingual dictionary is already available. Sanchez-Martinez et al. (2009) report that the MT accuracy is substantially higher for related languages, the proposed method exceeding even SMT systems (for which the parallel corpora used, averaging approximately one million words each, are found to be too small to allow effective linguistic modelling). Both aforementioned approaches have been combined with the Apertium[1] MT system.

Other MT systems have been proposed to cater for the case of low resources. Habash (2003) has proposed the Matador system for translation from Spanish to English, as a typical example of Generation-Heavy Machine Translation (GHMT), where resource poverty in the source language is addressed by exploiting TL resources. Carbonell et al. (2006) propose an MT method that requires no parallel text, but relies on a translation model utilising a full-form bilingual dictionary and a decoder using long-range context via large n-grams.

Another family of systems using low-cost resources encompasses METIS (Dologlou et al., 2003) and METIS-II (Markantonatou et al., 2009; Carl et al., 2008). These rely solely on extensive monolingual corpora in order to translate SL texts. METIS and METIS-II employ pattern recognition-based algorithms to determine the translation.

3 The PRESEMT system in brief

The architecture of PRESEMT has been formulated on the basis of experience collected within METIS and METIS-II. However, PRESEMT has been substantially modified in order to provide a measurable increase in translation speed and accuracy.

More specifically, in terms of resources, PRESEMT uses a bilingual dictionary providing SL – TL lexical correspondences. It also uses, as does METIS-II, an extensive TL monolingual corpus, which is compiled automatically via web crawling; a small bilingual corpus is yet additionally employed, in order to (a) reduce the number of possible translations that need to be evaluated by the system and (b) define examples of SL – TL structural modifications, thus improving the translation quality. The bilingual corpus need not cover a particular domain and only numbers a few hundred sentences (typically ~200) for determining structural equivalences between the source and target languages. Hence, in comparison to SMT systems, the size of the parallel corpus required is reduced by at least three orders of magnitude.

Both the bilingual and the monolingual corpora are annotated [2] with lemma and Part-of-Speech (PoS) information and, depending on the language, with additional morphological features (e.g. case, number, tense etc.). Furthermore, they are segmented into non-recursive syntactic phrases (e.g. noun phrase, verb phrase etc.). The next section details the kind of information extracted.

3.1 Exploiting the corpora

The processing of the bilingual corpus involves the combined use of two modules, the Phrase aligner module (PAM) and the Phrasing model generator (PMG). Details on PAM and PMG are provided in Tambouratzis et al. (2011), though their operation is summarised here for reasons of completeness.

Initially, the bilingual corpus is aligned at word and phrase level by PAM. PAM aims at circumventing incompatibilities of different annotation tools, based on a learning-by-example principle. It identifies how the SL structure is modified towards the TL one, allowing the deduction of a phrasing model for the source language. To operate, PAM assumes the existence of a parser in TL, which provides chunking information. Based on lexical information combined with statistical data on PoS tag correspondences drawn from the bilingual lexicon, PAM transfers the parsing scheme from the TL side of the corpus (bearing lemma, tag and parsing

[1] www.apertium.org

[2] For the annotation task readily available tools are employed, including statistical taggers and (to some extent) chunkers that provide shallow parsing. This alleviates the need for developing new linguistic tools.

information[3]), to the SL side, which is only tagged and lemmatised. In other words, the SL side is segmented into phrases in accordance to the phrasal segmentation provided for the TL side. PAM follows a three-step process, involving (a) lexicon-based correspondences, (b) alignment based on similarity of grammatical features and PoS tag correspondence and (c) alignment guided by already aligned neighbouring words. In each consecutive step, additional SL words are assigned to phrases, but with a reduced accuracy, the aim being for all words to be assigned to phrases.

The SL side of the aligned corpus is subsequently processed by PMG, with a two-fold purpose, namely to (i) deduce a phrasing model based on conditional random fields (CRF) (Lafferty et al., 2001) and (ii) employ this model for parsing any SL text submitted for translation.

The TL monolingual corpus serves as the basis for extracting two models, which are employed during the translation process. The first one is used solely for disambiguation purposes (cf. subsection 6.4). The second model provides the micro-structural information on the translation output to support word reordering. It derives from a phrase-based indexing of the TL monolingual corpus, which is performed offline during the pre-processing stage and is based on (i) phrase type, (ii) phrase head and (iii) phrase head PoS tag.

To implement a fast retrieval, the TL phrases are then organised in a hash map that allows the storage of multiple values for each key, using as a key the three aforementioned criteria. For each phrase the number of occurrences within the corpus is also retained. Each hash map is serialised and stored in a file with a unique name for immediate access by the search algorithm.

The number of files created as a result of this process is large, yet each of the files is of small size and thus can be loaded quickly. Furthermore, the existence of a given word in a phrase does not necessarily mean that this phrase will be grouped with other phrases containing the same word, since the model is based on the phrase head.

For the experiments reported here, the TL monolingual corpus is indexed based on the criteria listed above. However, a different indexing scheme may prove more effective, and thus experiments on the optimal indexing are continuing. For instance, the environment of the phrase may also be stored (i.e. the type of the previous and next phrases) and in this case the phrase organisation may be modified. These modifications may yield a decrease in computational load during translation, by reducing the number of phrase comparisons.

3.2 Main translation engine

The translation process is split into two phases, each of which makes use of only a single type of corpus. Phase 1 (**Structure selection**) uses the bilingual corpus to determine, for a given input SL sentence, the appropriate TL structure in terms of phrase type and order. The output of the Structure selection phase is the SL sentence with a TL structure, created by reordering the phrases according to the parallel corpus, and all words replaced by the TL lemmas and tag information as retrieved from the bilingual dictionary.

Phase 2 (**Translation equivalent selection**) uses the monolingual corpus to specify the most likely word order within phrases, to handle functional words such as articles and prepositions and to resolve lexical ambiguities emerging from the possible translations provided by the bilingual dictionary. Finally, a token generator component generates tokens out of lemmas. Therefore, the first PRESEMT translation phase is closely related to EBMT, while the second phase is reliant upon statistical information, resulting in a hybrid nature.

4 Example of the PRESEMT translation process

In this section the translation process of the PRESEMT system is illustrated via a simple example. Details on the algorithmic part are provided in the subsequent sections.

Input Sentence: Εδραιώνονται σχέσεις καλής γειτονίας στις χώρες των Βαλκανίων (= "Good neighbourhood relations are established in the Balkan countries")

Annotation at various levels [tagging & lemmatising; PMG-based segmentation to phrases; output of the lexicon look-up]

Input sentence annotation after being input for translation				
Phrase	**Word**	**Lemma**	**Tag**	**Lexicon**
VC[4]	εδραιώνονται	εδραιώνω	**vb**o3pl	{consolidate;

[3] For the experiments reported here, TreeTagger (Schmid, 1994) was used for the TL processing.

[4] VC: verb chunk, PC: prepositional chunk

Input sentence annotation after being input for translation				
Phrase	**Word**	**Lemma**	**Tag**	**Lexicon**
				establish}
PC	σχέσεις καλής γειτονίας	σχέση καλός γειτονία	**no**feplnm **aj**fesgge **no**fesgge	{relation; relationship} {nice; decent; good} {adjacency; neighbourhood}
PC	στις χώρες των Βαλκανίων	στου χώρα ο Βαλκάνια	**as**feplac **no**feplac **at**neplge **no**neplge	{on; at; to; into; in; upon} {country} {the} {Balkan}

1st translation phase: Establish the correct phrase order on the basis of TL. Search the bilingual corpus for the most similar SL sentence in structural terms, find the corresponding TL one and reorder the input sentence accordingly.

Most similar SL sentence of the bilingual parallel corpus			
Phrase	**Word**	**Lemma**	**Tag**
VC	σημειώνονται	σημειώνω	**vb**03pl
PC	διαμαρτυρίες φοιτητών	διαμαρτυρία φοιτητής	**no**feplnm **no**maplge
PC	σε άλλες χώρες της ΕΕ	σε άλλος χώρα ο ΕΕ	**aspp**sp **pn**fe03plac **no**feplac **at**ffesgge **abbr**
Corresponding TL sentence of the bilingual parallel corpus			
Phrase	**Word**	**Lemma**	**Tag**
PC	student protests	student protest	nn nns
VC	occur	occur	vv
PC	In other EU countries	in other EU country	in jj np nns

Output of 1st transl. phase (expressed as list of phrases and lemmas): [{relation; relationship}; {nice; decent; good}; {adjacency; neighbourhood} $_{PC}$] [{consolidate; establish} $_{VC}$] [{on; at; to; into; in; upon}; {country}; {the}; {Balkan} $_{PC}$]

2nd translation phase: Identify the correct word order within each phrase. Disambiguate the translations. Generate tokens out of lemmas

Word reordering results: [{nice; decent; good}; {adjacency; neighbourhood}; {relation; relationship} $_{PC}$] [{consolidate; establish} $_{VC}$] [{on; at; to; into; in; upon}; {the}; {Balkan}; {country} $_{PC}$]

Disambiguation: [{good}; {neighbourhood}; {relation} $_{PC}$] [{establish} $_{VC}$] [{in}; {the}; {Balkan}; {country} $_{PC}$]

Token generation: [{good}; {neighbourhood}; {relations} $_{PC}$] [{are established} $_{VC}$] [{in}; {the}; {Balkan}; {countries} $_{PC}$]

Final Translation: [Good neighbourhood relations $_{PC}$] [are established $_{VC}$] [in the Balkan countries $_{PC}$]

5 Phase 1: Structure selection

The task of Structure selection is to determine the type of TL phrases to which the SL ones translate and to order them in the TL sentence. To this end it consults the patterns of SL – TL structural modifications to be found in the parallel corpus, thus resembling EBMT (Hutchins, 2005).

Translation phase 1 receives as input an SL sentence (termed **ISS** – Input Source Sentence), bearing lexical translations from the dictionary, annotated with tag & lemma information and segmented into phrases by PMG. A dynamic programming algorithm then determines for each ISS the most similar, in terms of phrase structure, SL sentence found in the bilingual corpus (termed **ACS** – Aligned Corpus Sentence)[5].

The similarity is determined by taking into account structural information such as phrase type, phrase head PoS tag, phrase functional head info and phrase head case. The ISS phrases are then reordered in accordance to the TL side of the chosen ACS by replicating the SL-TL phrase alignment mapping. The data flow of the Structure selection is depicted in Figure 1.

The dynamic programming algorithm is essentially a monolingual similarity algorithm. The most similar SL structure of the bilingual corpus, that determines the TL structure of the sentence to be translated, is thus selected purely on SL properties. The implemented method is based on the Smith-Waterman algorithm (Smith and Waterman, 1981), initially proposed for alignment of DNA and RNA sequences. This algorithm is guaranteed to find the optimal local alignment between two input sequences.

[5] If the most similar ACS retrieved from the parallel corpus is very dissimilar, then ISS does not undergo any reordering. It is notable that in our experiments never did such an occasion appear, the similarity always reaching a high percentage (above 70%). The fact that comparisons involve sentences of the same language (SL) ensures a high similarity score.

5.1 Calculating structural similarity

The structural similarity between ISS and ACS is reflected on the similarity score, for the calculation of which a two-dimensional matrix is created with the ISS along the top row and the ACS along the left side. A cell *(i,j)* represents the similarity of the sub-sequence of elements up to the mapping of the elements E_i of the ACS and E'_j of the ISS, where each element corresponds to a phrase. The similarity for cell *(i,j)* is determined by examining the predecessor cells located directly to the left *(i, j-1)*, directly above *(i-1, j)* and above-left *(i-1, j-1)*, that contain values V1, V2 and V3 respectively, and is calculated iteratively as the maximum of the three numbers {max(V1, V2, V3)+ElementSimilarity(E_i, E'_j)}. The similarity of two phrases (PhrSim) is calculated as the weighted sum of four criteria, namely the similarities of (a) the phrase type (PhrTypSim), (b) the phrase head PoS tag (PhrHPosSim), (c) the phrase head case (PhrHCasSim) and (d) the functional phrase head PoS tag (PhrfHPosSim):

$$\begin{aligned} PhrSim(E_i,E'_j) = {} & W_{phraseType}*PhrTypSim(E_i,E'_j) + \\ & W_{headPoS}*PhrHPosSim(E_i,E'_j) + \\ & W_{headCase}*PhrHCasSim(E_i,E'_j) + \\ & W_{fheadPoS}*PhrfHPosSim(E_i,E'_j) \end{aligned}$$

For normalisation purposes, the sum of the four aforementioned weights (whose experimental values[6] are *0.4*, *0.1*, *0.1* and *0.4* respectively) is equal to *1*. The similarity score ranges from *100* to *0*, these limits denoting exact match and total dissimilarity between elements E_i and E'_j respectively. In case of a zero similarity score, a penalty weight (-50) is employed, to further penalise mapping of dissimilar items.

When the algorithm has reached the jth element of the ISS, the similarity score between the two SL sentences is calculated as the value of the maximum j^{th} cell. The ACS that achieves the highest similarity score is the closest to the input SL sentence in terms of phrase structure.

After determining the similarity between sentences, as the final similarity score, the comparison matrix indicates the optimal phrase alignment between the two SL sentences. By combining the SL sentence alignment from the algorithm with the alignment information between the ACS and the attached TL sentence, ISS phrases are reordered according to the TL side structure.

To illustrate this approach, an example is provided with Greek as SL and English as TL. Let us assume the ISS given in (1):

(1) Με τον όρο Μηχανική Μετάφραση αναφερόμαστε σε μια αυτοματοποιημένη διαδικασία (*"The term Machine Translation denotes an automated procedure"*)

The input sentence is segmented by PMG into the structure depicted in (2a); the structure elements being exemplified in (2b):

(2a) pc(as, no_ac) pc(-, no_ac) vp(-, vb) pc(as, no_ac)

(2b) <Phrase type> (<Phrase fhead PoS tag>, <Phrase head PoS tag>_<Phrase head case>)

An indicative ACS from the aligned corpus is given in (3):

(3) Οι ιστορικές ρίζες της Ευρωπαϊκής Ένωσης ανάγονται στο Δεύτερο Παγκόσμιο Πόλεμο. (*"The historical roots of the European Union lie in the Second World War"*)

The corresponding structural information for (3) is: pc(-,no_nm) pc(-,no_ge) vc(vb) pc(as,no_ac).

			Input source sentence (ISS)			
			pc (as, no_ac)	pc (-, no_ac)	vc (-, vb)	pc (-, no_ac)
		0	0	0	0	0
Aligned corpus sentence (ACS)	pc(-, no_nm)	0	60	80	-20	60
	pc(-, no_ge)	0	60	140	40	40
	vc(vb)	0	-50	10	240	140
	pc(as, no_ac)	0	100	30	-40	**340**

Table 1. Matrix defining phrase correspondence of sentences (1) and (3)

Then, the matrix of Table 1 is created to calculate the similarity scores between sentences (1) and (3) (cells forming the best aligned subsequence are highlighted). By choosing for each element the maximum similarity, the transformation cost is calculated (340 in this case). Based on this matrix, ISS is modified in accordance to the attached TL structure.

[6] An optimisation module has been designed as part of the PRESEMT system for defining the optimal values of these parameters (cf. subsection 5.3 for more details).

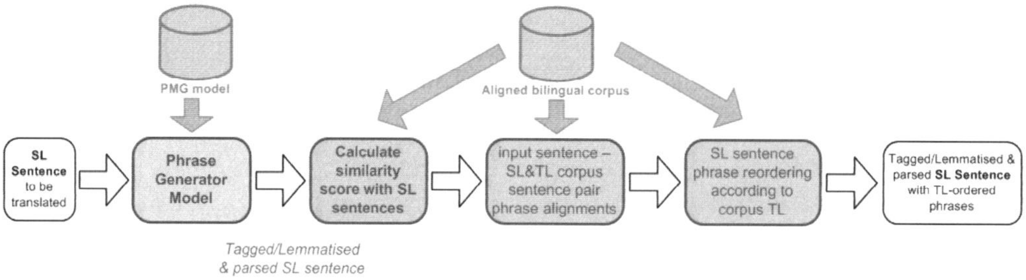

Figure 1. Data flow in Structure selection

6 Phase 2: Translation equivalent selection

Following Phase 1, the issues to be resolved in the second phase include (i) word ordering within phrases, (ii) handling of functional words and (iii) resolution of translation ambiguities.

6.1 Searching for phrasal equivalents

The monolingual TL corpus is searched to determine the most similar phrase to each phrase in the SL sentence, in order to establish the correct word order. The similarity measure takes into account the phrase type, and the words contained in the phrase in terms of lemma, PoS tag and morphological features. These factors enter the comparison with different weights, whose relative magnitudes are subject to an optimisation process.

The main issue at this stage is to reorder appropriately any items within each phrase. This entails that the words of a given phrase of the input sentence (denoted as **ISP –** Input Sentence Phrase), and the words of a retrieved TL phrase (denoted as **MCP** – Monolingual Corpus (TL) Phrase), are close to each other in terms of number and type. The data flow of the Translation equivalent selection is depicted in Figure 2.

6.2 Establishing correct word order

When initiating Phase 2 of the translation process, the matching algorithm accesses the indexed TL phrase corpus to retrieve similar phrases and select the most similar one through a comparison process, which is viewed as an assignment problem. This problem can be solved via algorithms such as the Gale-Shapley (Gale and Shapley, 1962; Mairson, 1992) and Kuhn–Munkres ones (Kuhn, 1955; Munkres, 1957). The Kuhn-Munkres approach computes an exact solution of the assignment problem to determine the optimal matching between elements. Experiments with METIS-II have shown that the solution of the assignment problem is computationally-intensive.

On the contrary, the Gale-Shapley algorithm solves the assignment problem in a reduced time. In this approach, the two sides are termed suitors (in PRESEMT, the SL side) and reviewers (the TL side). The two groups have distinct roles, suitors proclaiming their order of preference of being assigned to a specific reviewer, via an ordered list. Each reviewer selects one of the suitors after evaluating them based on the ordered preference list, in subsequent steps revising its selection so that the resulting assignment is improved. This process is suitor-optimal but possibly non-optimal from the reviewers' viewpoint. As its complexity is substantially lower than that of Kuhn-Munkres, the Gale-Shapley algorithm is adopted in PRESEMT to limit the computation time.

For each SL phrase, it is necessary to establish the correct word order for all possible TL phrases that can be produced by combining the lexical equivalents of each word in the phrase.

After the completion of this comparison process, the selected phrase from the monolingual corpus serves as a basis for resolving other issues such as the handling of functional words (e.g. insertion / deletion of articles). In this process, the TL information prevails over the SL entries.

6.3 Optimising the selection process of phrasal equivalents

The search for the most similar phrase depends on a set of parameters. Within this set, different types of weights are included, such as weights governing the similarity of PoS tags, lemmas, phrase types and morphological features. The weights from both translation phases are handled in a unified manner by the Optimisation module. Research in earlier MT systems has shown that the application of Genetic Algorithms (GAs) and multi-objective evolutionary algorithms such as SPEA2 (Improved Strength Pareto Evolutionary Algorithm) for the optimisation of parameters can considerably improve the translation quality (Sofianopoulos et al., 2010).

For the experiments presented in the next section, manually-defined preliminary weights are used for the parameters of both phases. To further improve the translation accuracy, an optimisation process is studied. This optimisation (which is beyond the scope of the present article) provides the prospect for a substantial improvement in the accuracy via the selection of appropriate parameter values.

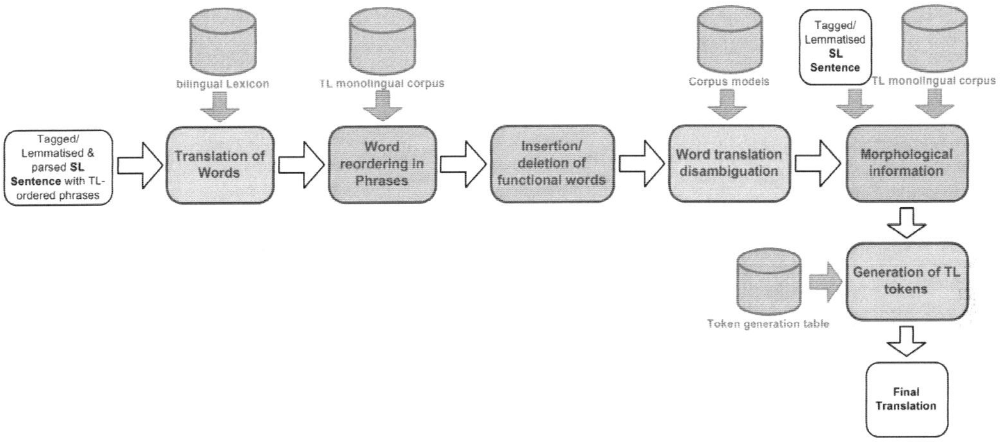

Figure 2. Data flow in Translation equivalent selection

6.4 Resolving translation ambiguities

Translation equivalent selection receives as input the output of Structure selection, which contains sets of candidate translations for each SL lemma. One translation needs to be chosen from each set, thus disambiguating amongst the possible translations. The disambiguation process uses the semantic similarities between words as evidenced by the monolingual corpus. Different approaches are evaluated for selecting the most appropriate translation, including Vector Space Modelling (Marsi et al., 2010) and Self-Organising Maps, following the work by Tsimboukakis et al. (2011).

These disambiguation processes lie beyond the scope of the present publication. On the contrary, a simpler, corpus-based approach is proposed here, which relies on the extraction of statistical information with only limited pre-processing. This method reuses and enhances the indexed sets of the monolingual corpus phrases, by exploiting information on the frequency of occurrence of each TL phrase. When searching for the best matching TL phrase for each combination of lexical alternatives, the frequency of the TL phrase is taken into account. Notably, not all combinations are examined for lexical disambiguation; instead only the phrase mapped to the most frequent TL phrase is retained.

7 Experimental Results

The evaluation results reported here concern the Greek – English language[7] pair and were based on the development datasets used in PRESEMT for studying the system performance. For each SL, these datasets contain 1,000 sentences, collected via web-crawling. Sentence length ranges from 7 to 40 words. From these datasets, 200 sentences were randomly chosen, and manually translated into each of the target languages. The correctness of these reference translations was checked independently by native speakers.

[7] PRESEMT handles 8 language pairs: SL {Czech, English, German, Greek, Norwegian} – TL {English, German}.

For the current evaluation phase four automatic evaluation metrics have been employed, i.e. BLEU (Papineni et al., 2002), NIST (NIST 2002), Meteor (Denkowski and Lavie, 2011) and TER (Snover et al., 2006). Table 2 summarises indicative scores obtained.

Number of sentences	40	Source		web
Reference translations	1	Language pair		EL – EN
MT system	Metrics			
	BLEU	NIST	Meteor	TER
PRESEMT 1	0.1297	4.1568	0.2669	79.417
PRESEMT 2	0.2004	4.9995	0.3294	72.678
Metis-II	0.1222	3.1655	0.2698	82.878
Google[8]	0.5472	7.1360	0.4713	29.963
Systran[9]	0.3143	5.4615	0.3857	49.449
WordLingo[10]	0.2908	5.1853	0.3728	49.632

Table 2. Evaluation results

When using the base PRESEMT system with the phrase-frequency disambiguation component deactivated (denoted as PRESEMT 1), a BLEU score of 0.1297 and a Meteor score of 0.2669 are obtained. When the disambiguation component is activated (PRESEMT 2), these scores increase substantially, reaching a BLEU score of just over 0.20. The BLEU improvement over PRESEMT 1 is 0.07 points (representing a 50% improvement), while NIST is increased by 0.85 and Meteor by over 0.06. TER is reduced by 7 points, also marking an improvement.

To put these scores into perspective, a comparison is made to MT systems available on the Internet, both rule-based (SYSTRAN) and SMT ones (Google Translate). In addition, the results of METIS-II are quoted, to compare PRESEMT with a system based on monolingual corpora. As can be seen, web-based MT systems produce higher scores for all metrics, with Google Translate possessing the best values.

Yet these scores are, especially in the case of Systran and WordLingo, not far off the scores obtained for PRESEMT with disambiguation. In particular NIST scores are directly comparable whilst the Meteor ones are not substantially higher. It can be reasonably assumed that due to the language-independent methodology without direct provision of language-specific information, the scores obtained via PRESEMT will be lower. Still, it is expected that refined versions of the PRESEMT algorithm will allow the achievement of higher scores that render its performance directly comparable to that of Systran and WordLingo, for the given language pair. In comparison to METIS-II, PRESEMT offers a substantial improvement for all metrics, with for instance BLEU and NIST scores increased by over 50%. This illustrates the improvements conferred by the new translation methodology. As noted, PRESEMT is still under development and it is anticipated that more extensive experiments involving additional language pairs will provide improvements in the translation quality.

8 Conclusions

In the present article the principles and the implementation of a novel language-independent methodology have been presented. The PRESEMT methodology draws on information residing in a large monolingual corpus and a small bilingual one for creating MT systems readily portable to new language pairs. Most of this information is extracted in an automated manner using pattern recognition techniques.

First experimental results using objective evaluation metrics and comparisons to established systems have also been reported. These results are promising, especially taking into account the fact that several PRESEMT modules are still under development and the translation process is being refined, in particular with respect to the handling of internal phrasal structure. These will be reported in future articles.

References

Michael Carl, Maite Melero, Toni Badia, Vincent Vandeghinste, Peter Dirix, Ineke Schuurman, Stella Markantonatou, Sokratis Sofianopoulos, Marina Vassiliou and Olga Yannoutsou. 2008. METIS-II: Low Resources Machine Translation: Background, Implementation, Results and Potentials. *Machine Translation, Vol. 22, No. 1-2*, pp. 67-99.

Jaime Carbonell, Steve Klein, David Miller, Michael Steinbaum, Tomer Grassiany, and Jochen Frey.

[8] translate.google.com
[9] www.systranet.com
[10] www.worldlingo.com

2006. Context-Based Machine Translation. In *Proceedings of the 7th Conference of the Association for Machine Translation in the Americas*, Cambridge, Massachusetts, USA, pp. 19-28.

Helena M. Caseli, Maria das Gracas V. Nunes, and Mikel L. Forcada (2008) Automatic Induction of Bilingual resources from aligned parallel corpora: Application to shallow-transfer machine translation. *Machine Translation, Vol. 20*, pp. 227-245.

Michael Denkowski and Alon Lavie. 2011. Meteor 1.3: Automatic Metric for Reliable Optimization and Evaluation of Machine Translation Systems. *EMNLP 2011 Workshop on Statistical Machine Translation*, Edinburgh, Scotland, pp. 85-91.

Ioannis Dologlou, Stella Markantonatou, George Tambouratzis, Olga Yannoutsou, Athanasia Fourla and Nikos Ioannou. 2003. Using Monolingual Corpora for Statistical Machine Translation: The METIS System. In Proceedings of the EAMT-CLAW'03 Workshop, Dublin, Ireland, pp. 61-68.

David Gale and Lloyd S. Shapley. 1962. College Admissions and the Stability of Marriage. *American Mathematical Monthly*, *Vol. 69*, pp. 9-14.

Declan Groves & Andy Way, 2005. Hybrid data-driven Models of Machine Translation. Machine Translation, Vol 19, pp.301-323.

Nizar Habash. 2003. Matador: A Large-Scale Spanish-English GHMT System. In *Proceedings of MT Summit IX*, New Orleans, LA, pp. 149-156.

John Hutchins. 2005. Example-Based Machine Translation: a Review and Commentary. *Machine Translation, Vol. 19*, pp.197-211.

Philip Koehn. 2010. *Statistical Machine Translation*. Cambridge University Press, Cambridge.

Harold W. Kuhn. 1955. The Hungarian method for the assignment problem. *Naval Research Logistics Quarterly*, *Vol. 2*, pp. 83-97.

John Lafferty, Andrew McCallum and Fernando Pereira. 2001. Conditional Random Fields: Probabilistic Models for Segmenting and Labelling Sequence Data. *28th International Conference on Machine Learning, ICML 2011*, Bellevue, Washington, USA, pp. 282-289.

Stella Markantonatou, Sokratis Sofianopoulos, Olga Giannoutsou and Marina Vassiliou. 2009. Hybrid Machine Translation for Low- and Middle-Density Languages. *Language Engineering for Lesser-Studied Languages, S. Nirenburg (ed.),* IOS Press, pp. 243-274.

Erwin Marsi, André Lynum, Lars Bungum, and Björn Gambäck. 2011. Word Translation Disambiguation without Parallel Texts. *International Workshop on Using Linguistic Information for Hybrid Machine Translation,* Barcelona, Spain, pp. 66-74.

Harry Mairson. 1992. The Stable Marriage Problem. *The Brandeis Review*, 12:1. Available at: www.cs.columbia.edu/~evs/intro/stable/writeup.html

James Munkres. 1957. Algorithms for the assignment and transportation problems. *Journal of the Society for Industrial and Applied Mathematics*, *Vol. 5*, pp. 32-38.

NIST 2002. Automatic Evaluation of Machine Translation Quality Using n-gram Co-occurrences Statistics.

Kishore Papineni, Salim Roukos, Todd Ward, and Wei-Jing Zhu. 2002. BLEU: A Method for Automatic Evaluation of Ma-chine Translation. *40th Annual Meeting of the Association for Computational Linguistics*, Philadelphia, USA, pp. 311-318.

Aaron Phillips. 2011. CUNEI: Open-source Machine Translation with Relevance-based models of each translation instance. Machine Translation, Vol. 25, pp. 161-177

Felipe Sanchez-Martinez and Mikel L. Forcada. 2009. Inferring Shallow-transfer Machine translation Rules from Small Parallel Corpora. *Journal of Artificial Intelligence Research, Vol. 34*, pp. 605-635.

Helmut Schmid. 1994. Probabilistic Part-of-Speech Tagging Using Decision Trees. In *Proceedings of International Conference on New Methods in Language Processing*, Manchester, UK, pp. 44-49.

Temple F. Smith and Michael S. Waterman. 1981. Identification of Common Molecular Subsequences. *Journal of Molecular Biology*, *Vol. 147*, pp. 195-197.

Matthew Snover, Bonnie Dorr, Richard Schwartz, Linnea Micciulla, and John Makhoul. 2006. A Study of Translation Edit Rate with Targeted Human Annotation. In *Proceedings of the 7th Conference of the Association for Machine Translation in the Americas*, Cambridge, Massachusetts, USA, pp. 223-231.

Sokratis Sofianopoulos, and George Tambouratzis. 2010. Multiobjective Optimisation of real-valued

Parameters of a Hybrid MT System using Genetic Algorithms. *Pattern Recognition Letters*, *Vol.* 31, pp.1672-1682.

George Tambouratzis, Fotini Simistira, Sokratis Sofianopoulos, Nikos Tsimboukakis, and Marina Vassiliou. 2011. A resource-light phrase scheme for language-portable MT. *15th International Conference of the European Association for Machine Translation*, Leuven, Belgium, pp. 185-192.

Nikos Tsimboukakis, and George Tambouratzis. 2011. Word map systems for content-based document classification. *IEEE Transactions on Systems, Man & Cybernetics – Part C, Vol. 41(5)*, pp. 662-673.

Language-Independent Named Entity Identification using Wikipedia

Mahathi Bhagavatula
Search and
Information Extraction Lab
IIIT Hyderabad
mahathi.b@research.iiit.ac.in

Santosh GSK
Search and
Information Extraction Lab
IIIT Hyderabad
santosh.gsk@research.iiit.ac.in

Vasudeva Varma
Search and
Information Extraction Lab
IIIT Hyderabad
vv@iiit.ac.in

Abstract

Recognition of Named Entities (NEs) is a difficult process in Indian languages like Hindi, Telugu, etc., where sufficient gazetteers and annotated corpora are not available compared to English language. This paper details a novel clustering and co-occurrence based approach to map English NEs with their equivalent representations from different languages recognized in a language-independent way. We have substituted the required language specific resources by the richly structured multilingual content of Wikipedia. The approach includes clustering of highly similar Wikipedia articles. Then the NEs in an English article are mapped with other language terms in interlinked articles based on co-occurrence frequencies. The cluster information and the term co-occurrences are considered in extracting the NEs from non-English languages. Hence, the English Wikipedia is used to bootstrap the NEs for other languages. Through this approach, we have availed the structured, semi-structured and multilingual content of the Wikipedia to a massive extent. Experimental results suggest that the proposed approach yields promising results in rates of precision and recall.

1 Introduction

Named entity recognition (NER) is an important subtask of information extraction that seeks to locate and classify atomic elements in text into predefined categories such as the names of persons, organizations, locations, etc.

The state-of-art NER systems for English produce near-human performance. However, for non-English languages the state-of-art NER systems perform below par. And for languages that have a lack of resources (e.g., Indian Languages) a NER system with a near-human performance is a distant future.

NER systems so far developed involved linguistic grammar-based techniques as well as statistical models. The grammar-based techniques require linguistic expertise and requires strenuous efforts to build a NER system for every new language. Such techniques can be safely avoided when there is a requirement to build a generic NER system for several languages (e.g., Indian Languages). Statistical NER systems typically require a large amount of manually annotated training data. With the serious lack of such manually annotated training data, the task of high-performance NER system projects as a major challenge for Indian languages.

This paper focuses on building a generic-purpose NE identification system for Indian languages. Given the constraints for resource-poor languages, we restrain from developing a regular NE Recognition system. However, the goal here is to identify as many NEs available in Indian languages without using any language-dependent tools or resources.

Wikipedia is a free, web-based, collaborative, multilingual encyclopedia. There are 283 language editions available as of now. Wikipedia has both structured (e.g., Infoboxes, Categories, Hyperlinks,

InterLanguage links, etc.) and semi-structured (content and organization of the page) information. Hence, the richly linked structure of Wikipedia present across several languages (e.g., English, Hindi, Marathi) has been used to build and enhance many NLP applications including NE identification systems. However, the existing approaches that exploit Wikipedia for recognizing NEs concentrates only on the structured parts which results in less recall. Our approach concentrates on exploiting structured and semi-structured parts of Wikipedia and hence yielding better results.

The approach used is simple, efficient, easily reproducible and can be extended to any language as it doesn't use any of the language specific resources.

2 Related Work

Wikipedia has been the subject of a considerable amount of research in recent years including Gabrilovich and Markovitch (2005), Milne et al. (2006), Zesch et al. (2007), Timothy Weale (2006) and Richman and Schone (2008). The most relevant work to this paper are Kazama and Torisawa (2007), Toral and Munoz (2006), Cucerzan (2007), Richman and Schone (2008). More details follow, however it is worth noting that all known prior research is fundamentally monolingual, often developing algorithms that can be adapted to other languages pending availability of the appropriate semantic resources.

Toral and Munoz (2006) used Wikipedia to create lists of NE's. They used the first sentence of Wikipedia articles as likely definitions of the article titles, and used them in attempting to classify the titles as people, locations, organizations, or none. Unlike the method presented in our paper, their algorithm relied on WordNet (or an equivalent resource in another language). The authors noted that their results would need to pass a manual supervision step before being useful for the NER task, and thus did not evaluate their results in the context of a full NER system.

Similarly, Kazama and Torisawa (2007) used Wikipedia, particularly the first sentence of each article, to create lists of entities. Rather than building entity dictionaries, associating words and phrases to the classical NE tags (PERSON, LOCATION, etc.), they used a noun phrase following the verb forms 'to be' to derive a label. For example, they used the sentence 'Franz Fischler ... is an Austrian politician' to associate the label 'politician' to the surface form 'Franz Fischler'. They proceeded to show that the dictionaries generated by their method are useful when integrated into an NER system. It is to be noted that their technique relies upon a part-of-speech tagger.

Cucerzan (2007), by contrast to the above, used Wikipedia primarily for Named Entity Disambiguation, following the path of Bunescu and Pasca (2006). As in our paper, and unlike the above mentioned works, Cucerzan (2007) made use of the explicit Category information found within Wikipedia. In particular, Category and related list derived data were key pieces of information used to differentiate between various meanings of an ambiguous surface form. Cucerzan (2007) did not make use of the Category information in identifying the class of a given entity. It is to be noted that the NER component was not the focus of their research, and was specific to the English language.

Richman and Schone (2008) emphasized on the use of links between articles of different languages, specifically between English (the largest and best linked Wikipedia) and other languages. The approach uses English Wikipedia structure namely categories and hyperlinks to get NEs and then use language specific tools to derive multilingual NEs.

The following are the majors differences between any of the above approaches to the approach followed in this paper.

- No language resource has been used at any stage of NE identification, unlike the above approaches that used at least one of the language dependent tools like dictionary, POS tagger,etc.
- Our approach utilized several aspects of Wikipedia (e.g., InterLanguage links, Cate-

gories, Sub-titles, Article Text), which has been by far the best exploitation of various structural aspects of Wikipedia.

- Language-independent mapping of multilingual similar content (i.e., the parallel/comparable topics or sentences of different languages) can be used as a reference to any future work. Further details can be found in the Section 4.2.

3 Wikipedia Structure

From Wikipedia, we exploited the following three major units:

Category links: These are the links from an article to 'Category' pages, represented in the form of [[Category:Luzerne County, Pennsylvania]], [[Category:Rivers of Pennsylvania]], etc.

InterLanguage links: Links from an article to a presumably equivalent article in another language. For example, in the English language article 'History of India', one finds a set of links including [[hi:भारतीय इतिहास]]. In almost all cases, the articles linked in this manner represent articles on the same subject.

Subtitles of the document: These are considered to be semi-structured parts of a Wikipedia article. Every page in Wikipedia consists of a title and subtitles. Considering the data below the subtitles, they can be referred as subparts of the article. For example, the article regarding Jimmy Wales has subtitles 'Early life and education', 'Career', etc.

4 Architecture

The system architecture involves 3 main steps and are detailed as follows:

4.1 Related Document Clustering:

Hierarchical clustering outputs a hierarchy, a structure that is more informative than the unstructured set of clusters returned by flat clustering. This paper deals with large amounts of semi-structured data and requires structured clusters as output rather than unstructured clusters. Moreover, specifying the number of clusters beforehand is difficult. Hence, we prefer Hierarchical clustering over Flat clustering in rest of the paper. Bottom-up algorithms can reach a cluster configuration with a better homogeneity than Top-Down clustering. Hence, we prefer bottom-up clustering over top-down clustering.

Within bottom-up clustering there are several similarity measures that can be employed namely single linkage, complete linkage, group average and centroid-measure. This single-link merge criterion is local. Priority is given solely to the area where the two clusters come closest to each other. Other, more distant parts of the cluster and the clusters' overall structure are not taken into account. In complete-link clustering or complete-linkage clustering, the similarity of two clusters is the similarity of their most dissimilar members. In centroid clustering, the similarity of two clusters is defined as the similarity of their centroids. Group-average agglomerative clustering or GAAC evaluates cluster quality based on all similarities between documents, thus avoiding the pitfalls of the single-link and complete-link criteria. Hence, in this paper, we made use of the Group-average agglomerative clustering.

We have considered the English Wikipedia articles which contain InterLanguage links to Hindi articles. The English articles are clustered based on the overlap of terms, i.e., the number of common terms present between articles. The clustering algorithm is detailed as follows:

Initially, consider English Wikipedia data, each article in the dataset is considered as a single document cluster. Now, the distance between two clusters is calculated using

$$\text{SIM-GA}(\omega_i, \omega_j) = \frac{1}{(N_i+N_j)(N_i+N_j-1)} \sum_{d_m \in \omega_i \cup \omega_j} \sum_{d_n \in \omega_i \cup \omega_j, d_m \neq d_n} \vec{d_m} \cdot \vec{d_n}$$

where $\vec{d}$ is the length-normalized vector of document d, $\cdot$ denotes the dot product, and N_i and N_j are the number of documents in ω_i and ω_j, respectively. Using group average agglomerative clustering, the process is repeated till we reach a certain threshold (set to 0.2) and thus the hierarchical clusters of English data are formed. In order to cluster documents of other languages, we availed the InterLanguage links and structure of English clusters. The InterLanguage links are used in replicating the cluster structure of English Wikipedia articles across other language articles. Therefore, we avoided the repetition of the clustering step for non-English articles. These different language clusters, being interconnected, are further utilized in our approach.

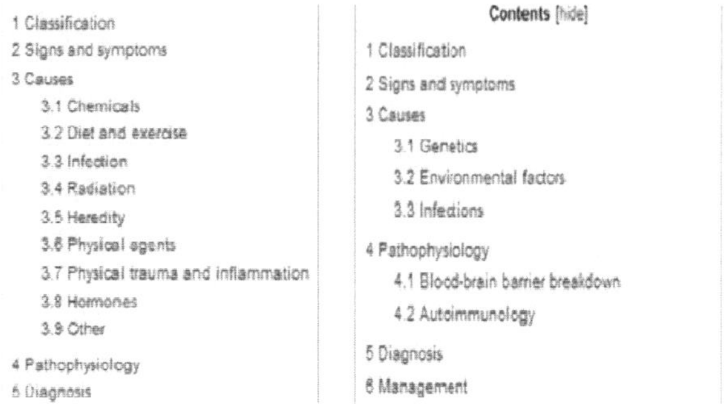

Figure 1: Subtitles of Cancer and Multiple Sclerosis

4.2 Mapping related content within interlinked documents:

As the clustering technique used is hierarchical, the intermediate clustering steps are gathered and are called as subclusters. For example, if two clusters (say Diseases, Hospitals) are merged to form a cluster (say Medicine). Then the Diseases, Hospitals are called subclusters for the Medicine cluster.

We measured the average of cosine similarities between the subtitle lists of the articles in a given cluster. If the average similarity exceeds a threshold (set to 0.72), it would mean the articles in the cluster (e.g., Diseases) all share similar subtitles. Otherwise, we go for a subcluster, until the threshold criteria is met. E.g., any two articles of the cluster Diseases share the common subtitles like Symptoms of Disease, Causes, Precautions, etc. This is illustrated in figure 1. As per our observation, the articles of different languages pertaining to same cluster will have same subtitles but depicted in different languages. The Hindi articles of cluster 'Diseases' share the same subtitles with those in English. This is illustrated in figure 2.

In order to map subtitles across languages, in each cluster, consider the non-English article with maximum number of subtitles and its corresponding English article. A lookup in a bilingual dictionary developed by Rohit et al. (2010) would help in mapping certain subtitles. The rest of the subtitles are mapped based on their order of occurrences. The subtitles are likely to occur at the same order in interlinked articles with high number of subtitles. The dictionary is expanded by adding the mapped subtitles obtained from such interlinked articles. This process is repeated with the remaining interlinked articles. Rohit et al. had developed the bilingual dictionary availing Wikipedia titles and abstract information. Hence, their approach is language-independent and doesn't hinder our algorithm from being applied to other languages.

Consider each subtitle of an article in a cluster and collect its subtitle data from that article and from its corresponding interlinked article in Hindi. For example, consider the subtitle 'Causes', collect the subtitle data from an English article (say Cancer) and map it with the subtitle data from the Hindi equivalent page on Cancer. We now have a mapping titled 'Causes - Cancer' for the Cancer articles across languages. Repeat this for all articles and group the mappings of common subtitles. Then, a major group 'Causes' is formed. This group will now have a set of mappings like 'Causes - Cancer', 'Causes - Multiple Sclerosis', etc. Thus the multilingual grouping and mapping is done. This step maps similar content of different languages. This is one of the important contributions of the paper which has the potential to be applied elsewhere.

4.3 Term co occurrences model:

Consider a map (e.g., 'Causes - Cancer') which contains both English and Hindi data. Given the fact that the usage of English tools doesn't hurt the extensibility of the approach to other languages, the English data is annotated with Stanford NER and the NEs are retrieved. Hindi data is preprocessed by removing the stop words. The stop words list is generated by considering words that occur above a certain frequency in the overall dataset.

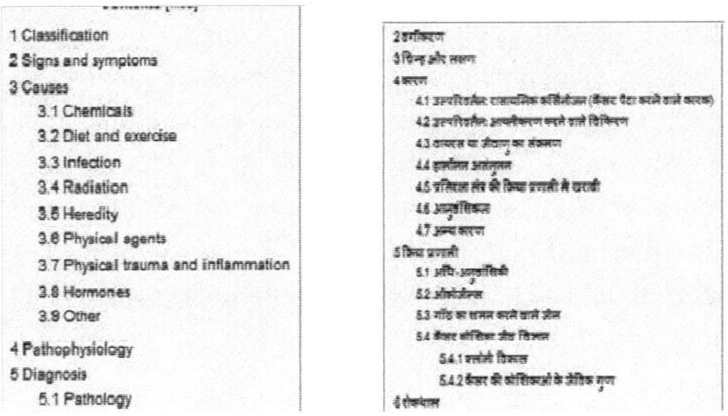

Figure 2: Subtitles of Cancer article across languages

For a given map and preprocessed data, every English NE is paired with every non-tagged Hindi word. Attach a default weight (=1) for each pair. Hence, a pair may look like (tagged English word, non tagged Hindi word, 1). This step is repeated with all other mappings present in a group (Ex: 'Causes - Cancer', 'Causes - Multiple Sclerosis' in the group 'Causes'). On repeated occurrence of the same pair, weight of that pair increases (by 1). Finally, for a English NE term, the Hindi term with which it has highest frequency is identified. Then the NE tag of English term is assigned to Hindi term. Hence, Hindi word is labeled. This step is repeated with the remaining English NEs and Hindi terms.

For example, consider two small mappings, each with two English NEs and one sentence in Hindi. Consider the first map, with "Alexander/PERSON", "India/LOCATION" as English NEs and एलेक्जेंडर ने भारत में पंजाब तक के प्रदेश पर विजय हासिल की थी। as Hindi sentence. Then each NE of English is attached with each Hindi word (except the stop words) like Alexander - एलेक्जेंडर, Alexander - भारत, Alexander - पंजाब, India - एलेक्जेंडर, etc., in all combinations. Consider the second map with 'Alexander/PERSON', 'Philip/PERSON' as English NEs and एलेक्जेंडर के पिता का नाम फिलीप था। as Hindi sentence. The pairs would be Alexander - एलेक्जेंडर, Alexander - फिलीप etc. Hence, the maximum co occurred pair would be Alexander - एलेक्जेंडर (Alexander in Hindi). Then the NE tag of Alexander/PERSON is attached to एलेक्जेंडर/PERSON. Similarly, for the remaining English NEs and Hindi terms, the maximum co-occurred pair is identified and the Hindi term is tagged.

5 Evaluation and Experimental setup:

As our approach requires InterLanguage links, we are only interested in a subset of English and Hindi Wikipedia articles which are interconnected. There are 22,300 articles in English and Hindi Wikipedia that have InterLanguage links. The output of Hierarchical GAAC clustering on this subset was observed to be 345 clusters. We have manually tagged Hindi articles of 50 random clusters (as cluster size can dictate accuracies) with three NE tags (i.e., Person, Organization, Location), resulting in 2,328 Hindi articles with around 11,000 NE tags. All further experiments were performed on this tagged dataset. Precision, Recall and F-measure are the evaluation metrics used to estimate the performance of our system.

In order to compare our system performance with a baseline, we have availed the Hindi NER system developed by Gali et al. (2008) at LTRC (Language Technologies Research Center) [1] that recognizes and annotates Hindi NEs in a given text using Conditional Random Fields (CRF) as the sequential labeling mechanism. Their system is reproduced on our dataset with a 5-fold cross validation using spell variations, pattern of suffixes and POS tagging as the features.

6 Experiments and Results:

The experiments conducted are broadly classified as follows:

Experiment 1: Using the structure of Wikipedia namely Category terms, we can cluster the articles which are having similar category terms. Another approach for clustering is to consider the Wikipedia page as an unstructured page and then cluster the articles based on the similarity of words present in it. We have performed Hierarchical GAAC based clustering for these experiments.

Experiment 2: Different clustering metrics will yield different accuracies for a given data. Here, we will measure which similarity metric is appropriate

[1] http://ltrc.iiit.ac.in

for the dataset under study following a Category information based clustering of articles.

6.1 Experiment 1: Whether to use structure of the Wikipedia page:

No_Category: *Clustering without using the Category information:* As the first experiment, the articles are clustered based on the article text and not using the category terms.

With_Category: *Clustering using the Category information:* In this experiment, the category terms are used for clustering the documents. The F-measure suggests that category terms better capture the semantics of an article when compared to the text of the article. Adding to the fact that category terms suggest a compact representation of an article whereas the text include noisy terms. The compact representation of articles has proved to be crucial by our next set of experiments.

	Precision	Recall	F-measure
NER_LTRC	64.9	50.6	56.81
No_Category	69.8	62.7	66.05
With_Category	73.5	64.3	68.59

Table 1: Experiment to determine the impact of structure based clustering

6.2 Experiment 2: Similarity metrics for Clustering

SLAC: *Single-linkage Agglomerative Clustering:* Single-linkage algorithm would make use of minimum distance between the clusters as similarity metric. One of the drawback for this measure is that if we have even a single document related to two clusters, the clusters are merged. In Wikipedia, we will not have un-related documents, all the documents will be having a certain overlap of terms with each other. Hence, the number of clusters formed are relatively less compared to other two similarity measures. Thus the measures of Precision, Recall and F-measure are quite less.

CLAC: *Complete-linkage Agglomerative Clustering:* Complete-linkage algorithm would make use of maximum distance between the clusters as similarity metric. This results in a preference for compact clusters with small diameters over long. Hence, the accuracies are improved. The drawback is that it causes sensitivity to outliers.

GAAC: *Group Average Agglomerative Clustering:* Group Average is the average between single-linkage metric and complete-linkage metric. Hence, covers the advantages of the both, overcoming the drawbacks of both metrics to some extent. Thus, the accuracies have improved considerably over previous experiments.

	Precision	Recall	F-measure
NER_LTRC	64.9	50.6	56.81
SLAC	67.6	60.3	63.74
CLAC	70.3	61.1	65.38
GAAC	73.5	64.3	68.59

Table 2: Experiment to evaluate similarity metrics

7 Discussions:

From the above results, we have made the following observations. (I) Experiment 1: The Category information of Wikipedia was able to capture the semantics and represent the articles in a compact way resulting in higher accuracies over the article text information. (II) Experiment 2: As each cluster is processed independently while identifying NEs, the compactness and uniformity of the clusters matter in our approach. This is studied by considering different similarity metrics while forming clusters. Finally, from the experiments we conclude that formation of hard clusters matter more for better results of the approach.

8 Conclusions

This paper proposes a method to identify the NEs in Indian languages for which the availability of resources is a major concern. The approach suggested is simple, efficient, easily reproducible and can be extended to any other language as it is developed under a language-independent framework. Wikipedia pages across languages are merged together at subtitle level and then the non-English NEs are identified based on term-term co-occurrence frequencies. The experimental results conclude that the use of Category information has resulted in compact representations and the compactness of the clusters plays a predominant role in determining the accuracies of the system.

References

Daniel M. Bikel and Richard Schwartz and Ralph M. Weischedel 1999. *An Algorithm that Learns What's in a Name*, volume 34. Journal of Machine Learning Research.

Silviu Cucerzan 2007. *Large-scale named entity disambiguation based on Wikipedia data.* In Proc. 2007 Joint Conference on EMNLP and CNLL, pages 708–716.

Evgeniy Gabrilovich and Shaul Markovitch 2007. *Computing semantic relatedness using Wikipedia-based explicit semantic analysis.* In Proceedings of the 20th International Joint Conference on Artificial Intelligence, pages 1606–1611.

Evgeniy Gabrilovich and Shaul Markovitch 2006. *Overcoming the brittleness bottleneck using wikipedia: enhancing text categorization with encyclopedic knowledge.* proceedings of the 21st national conference on Artificial intelligence - Volume 2, pages 1301–1306.

Evgeniy Gabrilovich and Shaul Markovitch 2005. *Feature generation for text categorization using world knowledge.* In IJCAI05, pages 1048–1053.

Jun'ichi Kazama and Kentaro Torisawa 2007. *Exploiting Wikipedia as External Knowledge for Named Entity Recognition.* Joint Conference on Empirical Methods in Natural Language Processing and Computational Natural Language Learning, pages 698–707.

David Milne and Olena Medelyan and Ian H. Witten 2006. *Mining Domain-Specific Thesauri from Wikipedia: A Case Study.* Proceedings of the 2006 IEEE/WIC/ACM International Conference on Web Intelligence, pages 442–448.

Antonio Toral and Rafael Munoz 2006. *A proposal to automatically build and maintain gazetteers for named entity recognition by using Wikipedia.* In EACL 2006.

Timothy Weale 2006. *Utilizing Wikipedia Categories for Document Classification.* Evaluation, pages 4.

Torsten Zesch and Iryna Gurevych and Max Mühlhäuser 2007. *Analyzing and Accessing Wikipedia as a Lexical Semantic Resource.* Biannual Conference of the Society for Computational Linguistics and Language Technology.

Alexander E. Richman and Patrick Schone 2008. *Mining Wiki Resources for Multilingual Named Entity Recognition.* ACL08.

Razvan Bunescu and Marius Pasca 2006. *Using Encyclopedic Knowledge for Named Entity Disambiguation.* EACL'06.

Karthik Gali and Harshit Surana and Ashwini Vaidya and Praneeth Shishtla and Dipti M Sharma. 2008 *Aggregating Machine Learning and Rule Based Heuristics for Named Entity Recognition.* IJCNLP'08.

Rohit Bharadwaj G, Niket Tandon and Vasudeva Varma. 2010 *An Iterative approach to extract dictionaries from Wikipedia for under-resourced languages.* ICON'10.

The Study of Effect of Length in Morphological Segmentation of Agglutinative Languages

Loganathan Ramasamy and **Zdeněk Žabokrtský**
Institute of Formal and Applied Linguistics
Faculty of Mathematics and Physics, Charles University in Prague
{ramasamy, zabokrtsky}@ufal.mff.cuni.cz

Sowmya Vajjala
Seminar für Sprachwissenschaft
Universität Tübingen
sowmya@sfs.uni-tuebingen.de

Abstract

Morph length is one of the indicative feature that helps learning the morphology of languages, in particular agglutinative languages. In this paper, we introduce a simple unsupervised model for morphological segmentation and study how the knowledge of morph length affect the performance of the segmentation task under the Bayesian framework. The model is based on (Goldwater et al., 2006) unigram word segmentation model and assumes a simple prior distribution over morph length. We experiment this model on two highly related and agglutinative languages namely Tamil and Telugu, and compare our results with the state of the art Morfessor system. We show that, knowledge of morph length has a positive impact and provides competitive results in terms of overall performance.

1 Introduction

Most of the NLP tasks require one way or another the handling of morphology. The task becomes very crucial when the language in question is morphologically rich as is the case in many Indo-European languages. The application of morphology is evident in applications such as Statistical Machine Translation (SMT) (Lee, 2004), dependency parsing, information retrieval and so on. Apart from the morphological analysis as in the traditional linguistic sense, morphological segmentation is also widely used as an easy alternative to full fledged morphological analysis. In this paper we mainly focus on the task of morphological segmentation.

The main task in morphological segmentation is to segment the given *token* or *wordform* into set of morphs or identifying the location of each morpheme boundary within the *token*. Morphological segmentation is most suitable for agglutinative languages (such as Finnish or Turkish) than fusional languages (such as Semitic languages).

Though both supervised (Koskenniemi, 1983) and unsupervised methods (Goldsmith, 2001; Creutz and Lagus, 2005) are extensively studied for morphological segmentation, unsupervised techniques have the appeal of application to multilingual data with cost effective manner. Within unsupervised paradigm, various methods have been explored. Minimum Description Length (MDL) (Goldsmith, 2001; Creutz and Lagus, 2005) based approaches are most popular in which the best segmentation corresponds to the compact representation of morphology and the resulting lexicon. (Goldwater et al., 2009; Snyder and Barzilay, 2008) attempted word segmentation and joint segmentation of related languages using Bayesian approach. (Demberg, 2007; Dasgupta and Ng, 2007) applied various probabilistic measures to discover affixes of wordforms. (Naradowsky and Goldwater, 2009; Yarowsky and Wicentowski, 2000) explored ways to model orthographic rules of wordforms.

In this work, we are mainly going to focus on Bayesian approach. Bayesian approaches provide natural way of modeling subjective knowledge as well as separating problem specific aspects from general aspects. In the case of agglutinative languages, the number of morphemes in a word as well as morph length play a major role in morphological process. The main rationale for this work is to study linguistic factors (mainly *morph length*), so that language specific priors can be applied over different languages. This will especially be useful when modeling resource poor languages (RPL) with little or no data, as well as building resources for RPL from resource rich languages (RRL).

Towards that objective, our main contribution in this work is, we introduce a simple unsupervised segmentation model based on Bayesian approach and we study the effect of morph length prior for two agglutinative languages.

2 Previous Work

In this section, we briefly survey earlier works that utilized the morph length information, then we provide basis for our unsupervised morphological segmentation model and finally we list some prior works on morphological analysis/segmentation of Telugu and Tamil.

Snover (2001) used an exponential like distribution for morph length that decreased over word length, thus favoring shorter morph lengths. Our work is directly related to (Creutz, 2003) as it made use of prior distributions on morph length and frequency of morphs under maximum a posteriori (MAP) framework. Gamma distribution was used as a prior distribution for morph length. The main difference between (Creutz, 2003) and our work is that, we are going to experiment different morph lengths under Bayesian framework.

Naradowsky (2011) introduced an exponential length penalty to prevent the model from under segmentation results. It also emphasized that avoiding length penalty seriously affected the model. (Poon et al. , 2009) indirectly specified about the morph length by restricting the number of morphemes per word.

In this work, we mainly rely on Goldwater (2009; 2006) which conducted an extensive study on the application of Bayesian approach to word segmentation in child-directed speech utterances. It included both unigram and bigram models (based on Hierarchical Dirichlet Processes) for word segmentation. Gibbs sampling was used to extract samples (utterances with word boundaries) from posterior distribution. We apply the unigram model (Goldwater et al., 2009) to morphological segmentation where the word boundaries in speech utterances correspond to morpheme boundaries in wordforms.

Before we describe unsupervised morphological segmentation model, we briefly survey the existing work on Telugu and Tamil morphological segmentation/analysis.

Rao et al. (2011) described in detail, the preparation of a linguistic database for Telugu morphological analysis, compiling 2800 morphological categories and reported a coverage of 95-97%. They followed a word and paradigm model, which was considered to be better suited for agglutinative languages. The issue of out-of-vocabulary words was handled better in the rule based approach by (Ganapathiraju and Levin, 2006). They describe a rule-based morphological analyzer *TelMore* for Telugu nouns and verbs.

Aksharbharathi et al. (2004) describes the development of a generic morphological analysis shell that uses dictionaries along with Finite State Transducers based feature structures, to perform the morphological analysis of a word. The feature structures were derived from the standard rules of the grammar in respective languages. This was tested with Hindi, Telugu, Tamil and Russian.

Kiranmai et al. (2010) describe a supervised morphological analyzer with support vector machines.

For Tamil, morphological segmentation is rarely studied. Most of the work is done for morphological analysis of wordforms. Most of the analyzers use rule based approaches. Dhanalakshmi et al. (2009) used sequence labeling approach to morphological analysis of wordforms.

3 Unsupervised Morphological Segmentation

Consider a wordform (w) of length n composed of characters from alphabet L_A,

$$w = c_1 c_2 c_3 ... c_n$$

The main objective is to identify the character positions where morpheme boundaries occur. The model we describe here is similar to the *cache model* described in (Goldwater et al., 2006) for word segmentation. We apply the same model to identify morpheme boundaries. The model makes decision at every character position in the wordform for the entire corpus. The hypothesis probability that no morpheme boundary at position i in wordform w is calculated as follows,

$$P(w_i^-|h) = \frac{n_{m_a} + \alpha P_0(m_a)}{N_m + \alpha} \quad (1)$$

m_a is a substring or a morph in the wordform w which contains the character position position i. n_{m_a} refers to number of times the morph m_a occurs in the history of morph counts N_m. In the case of having a boundary at position i, we will have two morphs to consider, one morph (m_a) to the left of position i (including i), and another morph (m_b) starting after i. The probability of having a morpheme boundary at position i is calculated in the same way as Equation 1, but this time with two morphs,

$$P(w_i^+|h) = \frac{n_{m_a} + \alpha P_0(m_a)}{N_m + \alpha} \cdot \frac{n_{m_b} + I(m_a == m_b) + \alpha P_0(m_b)}{(N_m + 1) + \alpha} \quad (2)$$

$I(m_a == m_b)$ takes the value 1 if both morphs are same, otherwise the value is 0. Also note that the additional 1 (due to previous factor) in the denominator of the second part of the equation. In both the equations, P_0 is a base distribution which can be utilized to put a bias over certain hypotheses. In our case, the base distribution (P_0) mainly assigns probability distribution over morph length. Additional linguistic factors can also be modeled this way. α is a *concentration parameter* which can be used to control P_0. Overall, the model (in equation 1 and 2) uses only unigram morph counts.

Every character position (except the last position) in a given word is a potential candidate that can have a morpheme boundary. To determine whether they really have morpheme boundary or not, for every character position i in w, we calculate hypothesis probabilities b_i^+ (i.e. has a morpheme boundary) and b_i^- (has no morpheme boundary). Having calculated the hypothesis probabilities, we choose the hypothesis by using a weighted coin flip. In our problem, we have only two hypotheses: (i) a morpheme boundary and (ii) no morpheme boundary. If the new hypothesis is different from the character's previous status, then appropriate data structures are updated. This procedure is repeated for many number of iterations.

3.1 Modeling morpheme length

We encode our beliefs about morph length via base distribution P_0. We chose *Poisson* distribution for modeling the length of the morphs. Poisson distribution utilizing morph length is defined as $P(l, k) = \frac{l^k e^{-l}}{k!}$, where l is an expected length of the morph and when supplied k, it returns the probability density of a morph having length k. We define two base distributions based on morph length prior,

$$P_0^A(m) = p(l, k) = \frac{l^k e^{-l}}{k!} \quad (3)$$

$$P_0^B(m) = p(m)p(l, k) = \frac{n_m}{\mid l_m \mid} \frac{l^k e^{-l}}{k!} \quad (4)$$

$p(m)$ is probability of the morph itself. $\mid l_m \mid$ - total number of substrings of length equal to the length of morph m. Morfessor (Creutz and Lagus, 2005) uses Zipfian distribution for frequencies and *gamma length prior* for modeling the length of the morphs. Setting a particular expected morph length effectively puts a bias towards that particular *morph length (l)*. We experiment both our base distributions over different morph lengths.

3.2 Inferencing

Gibbs sampling (Gilks et al., 1996) uses iterative procedure to repeatedly draw value of a variable given the current state of all other variables in the model. In our case, drawing a value is equal to determining whether there is a boundary at the character position, thus obtaining individual morphemes. We iteratively segment the given corpus or list of words into morphological segments. The intuitive idea is that, when we sample enough number of times i.e. drawing morphological segments of words given history of segments of all other words, the sampler converges to the posterior distribution of the morphological segments of the entire corpus. The Algorithm 1 gives a general outline of how the Gibbs sampling procedure is applied to morphological segmentation.

Algorithm 1: Basic Sampling Procedure

Data: words, model
Result: Segmented words
begin
  $RandSeg \longleftarrow InitializeSegments(words)$
  $Baseline \longleftarrow Evaluate(RandSeg)$
  $CurrSeg \longleftarrow RandSeg$
  $MorphCounts \longleftarrow GetCounts(CurrSeg)$
  for $i \in iterations$ **do**
    for $j \in size(words)$ **do**
      for $k \in length(words[j])$ **do**
        $b_k^- \longleftarrow Calculate(P(words[j]_k^-))$
        $b_k^+ \longleftarrow Calculate(P(words[j]_k^+))$
        if $HasNoBoundaryAt(k)$ **then**
          add boundary at k with probability $\frac{b_k^+}{b_k^- + b_k^+}$
          no change at k with probability $\frac{b_k^-}{b_k^- + b_k^+}$
        if $HasBoundaryAt(k)$ **then**
          remove boundary at k with probability $\frac{b_k^-}{b_k^- + b_k^+}$
          no change at k with probability $\frac{b_k^+}{b_k^- + b_k^+}$
        $UpdateCurrSeg(CurrSeg)$
        $AdjustMorphCounts(MorphCounts)$

We use *temperature (T)* settings (not shown in the algorithm) to make the sampling procedure converge faster. We use 10 values (from 0.1 to 1.0) for T and raise the probability values of hypotheses to $(\frac{1}{T})$. Also, we make the *collection rate* very small, so that only few and substantially different samples (or morphological segmentation of the entire corpus) are collected.

4 Experimental Setup

The experiments are carried out for the unigram segmentation model (*unsup-uni*) as described in Section 3 and Morfessor system (Creutz and Lagus, 2005). For both Tamil and Telugu, we perform the following experiments: (i) baseline (ii) *unsup-uni* with base distribution P_0^A (*unsup-uni-p0-len*) (iii) *unsup-uni* with base distribution P_0^B (*unsup-uni-p0-lex-len*) and (iv) with Morfessor. For each system, we add some knowledge about morph length (l) and report the accuracy.

The experiments (ii), (iii) and (iv) use additional dataset known as *extra-data. Extra-data* is an unannotated/unsegmented data which augments the *test data* while training the systems. As *test data* with gold segmentation is very small, we feel this step is necessary to make the evaluation credible. The following subsection describes the datasets in detail.

Baseline system corresponds to random segmentation. We evaluate *baseline* system for morph lengths 1 to 10. For each morph length (l) experiment, we change the probability of adding a boundary at each character position to be $(\frac{1}{l})$ except at $l = 1$ where the probability is 0.75.

Unsup-uni-p0-len experiment uses base distribution P_0^A (see Section 3.1). We conduct this experiment in 2 steps: (i) running the Gibbs sampler with the *extra-data* and (ii) use the parameters (including morph counts) from step (i) and run the Gibbs sampler on *test data*. We set the expected morph length (l) in the base distribution P_0^A every time we run the experiment for different morph length. For the step (i), the Gibbs sampler is run for 10000 iterations with different *concentration parameter* (α). We collect samples every 1000 iterations and we store the last sample as our model along with other parameters. For step (ii), we use the model from step (i) and run the Gibbs sampler on *test data*. We collect the final sample as our predicted segmentation of the *test data* and perform evaluation on the predicted segmentation. In *unsup-uni-p0-lex-len* experiment, we use the base distribution P_0^B (see Section 3.1). P_0^B includes morpheme probability apart from the length prior. Experiments for *unsup-uni-p0-lex-len* is carried out in the same way as that of *unsup-uni-p0-len*.

We use *gamma distribution* length prior for experiments with Morfessor. We train Morfessor on *extra-data* for morph lengths 1 to 10. We change the expected length in the gamma prior for each morph length experiment. Then we run the Morfessor on *test data* with same parameters created during the training.

We use *Precision (P), Recall (R)* and *F-score (F)*

Lang.	Words	Chars	Morphs	Avg. m.(l)
Tamil	1500	12642	3280	3.85
Telugu	998	10303	1733	5.95

Table 1: Gold segmentation: statistics

for evaluating our predicted segmentation with gold segmentation. Our evaluation is same as (Creutz and Lindén, 2004).

4.1 Data

We use EMILLE corpus (Xiao et al. , 2004) for our experiments. The EMILLE corpus contains monolingual, parallel and annotated data for various Indian languages. We randomly selected articles from *monolingual* section of Tamil and Telugu data. The original data were in `utf-8` and we transliterated the data into `latin` format. The transliteration step is an important step as it avoids confusion in specifying *morph length (l)*. As we already mentioned earlier, we use two sets (*extra-data* and *test data*) of data for each language. For training of *extra-data*, we use 30000 unique words list for each language. For *test data*, we make words list from real sentences thus it can contain multiple occurrences of a same wordform. The Table 1 provides the statistics of the *test data* for which we have manually performed gold segmentations. At present, our gold segmentation does not take into account multiple possible segmentations.

The Figure 1 shows morph counts distribution of both Tamil and Telugu (derived from gold segments) according to their morph lengths. Tamil has more morphs that are shorter in length than Telugu.

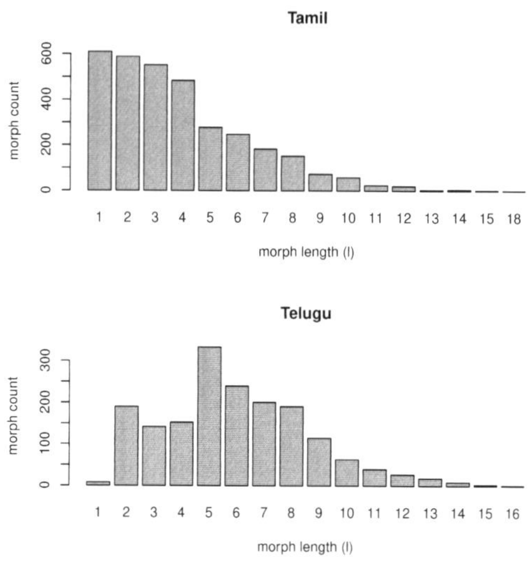

Figure 1: Morph counts according to morph length (l)

5 Results

The Table 2 shows evaluation results for the experimental setup described in the previous section.

For Tamil, most of the morphs have the length 1-4. The models *unsup-uni-p0-len* and *unsup-uni-p0-lex-len* perform quite well near to that length range. For the same range (l = 1 to 4), both the models together perform better than Morfessor in terms of F-score. The performance of *unsup-uni-p0-len* and *unsup-uni-p0-lex-len* are constantly decreasing and start to perform worse than Morfessor after length 5. This is somewhat expected that *unsup-uni* models are quite sensitive to length priors and may perform poorly if we assume morph lengths far from the true range. Whereas, Morfessor has a consistent performance over the entire length range (l = 1 to 10). This implies that, Morfessor is less sensitive to length priors even if we drastically change the expected morph length. *Unsup-uni-p0-len* gave the best overall performance (F-score - 48.83%) compared to other models in this task.

Telugu's common morph length ranges from 2-8. Except at l = 1 & 2, Morfessor beats both *unsup-uni-p0-len* and *unsup-uni-p0-lex-len* in all other remaining length ranges. *Unsup-uni* models perform quite poorly over different length ranges when comparing with Tamil for the same range. In this task, Morfessor's overall performance (F-score 43.63%) is better than *unsup-uni* models. Morfessor also performs better near the most frequent morph length range (5-8).

6 Some Observations on (l)

- The results (Table 2) suggest that *unsup-uni* model is quite sensitive to morph length parameter in the prior distributions.

- For Tamil, *unsup-uni* model performs well near to the true morph length range. But the performance deteriorates when the expected morph length parameter is too different from

Language	System	P/R/F	Morph length *(l)*									
			1	*2*	*3*	*4*	*5*	*6*	*7*	*8*	*9*	*10*
Tamil	baseline	P	15.79	15.86	17.04	17.11	15.33	16.33	15.98	14.75	17.63	16.65
		R	73.98	50.08	34.92	26.25	19.64	15.50	13.82	11.47	12.31	10.24
		F	26.02	24.09	22.91	20.72	17.22	15.91	14.82	12.91	14.50	12.68
	unsup-uni-p0-len	P	63.61	62.17	67.99	69.68	69.22	72.77	72.29	68.70	66.73	64.08
		R	39.62	40.01	36.49	33.18	28.82	26.47	24.23	22.10	20.65	20.76
		F	**48.83**	*48.69*	*47.49*	*44.96*	40.7	38.82	36.30	33.45	31.54	31.36
	unsup-uni-p0-lex-len	P	46.51	59.48	63.79	63.69	56.10	54.58	50.29	48.18	45.99	50.39
		R	41.35	41.07	39.34	38.28	36.04	33.69	34.25	34.08	33.02	28.65
		F	43.78	*48.59*	*48.67*	*47.82*	43.88	41.66	40.75	39.92	38.44	36.53
	Morfessor	P	48.54	48.32	48.61	49.01	50.24	49.07	49.93	49.21	49.42	48.93
		R	41.75	40.18	40.07	40.24	40.46	39.84	40.35	39.84	40.40	39.62
		F	44.89	43.87	43.93	44.19	44.82	43.98	44.63	44.03	44.64	43.78
Telugu	baseline	P	07.88	08.05	07.91	07.38	07.70	07.54	07.62	08.52	08.96	07.91
		R	75.69	51.59	32.97	23.86	20.00	16.00	13.66	13.38	12.97	10.07
		F	14.28	13.93	12.76	11.27	11.12	10.25	09.78	10.41	10.60	10.07
	unsup-uni-p0-len	P	36.67	37.29	36.2	39.71	41.87	40.58	41.34	39.15	38.10	33.65
		R	53.10	51.17	48.14	38.07	29.1	19.31	16.14	11.45	11.03	9.66
		F	43.38	43.14	41.33	38.87	34.34	26.17	23.21	17.72	17.11	15.01
	unsup-uni-p0-lex-len	P	22.27	26.55	32.46	35.76	28.29	19.31	19.83	18.3	18.17	17.26
		R	66.9	58.34	44.41	35.17	35.31	55.17	42.21	49.79	55.45	52.28
		F	33.41	36.5	37.51	35.47	31.41	28.6	26.98	26.76	27.37	25.95
	Morfessor	P	29.32	29.59	30.48	30.72	30.88	30.85	31.31	30.34	29.88	30.40
		R	70.30	69.48	69.48	69.75	70.17	70.30	71.96	70.99	70.58	71.96
		F	41.38	41.50	42.38	42.65	42.89	42.88	**43.63**	42.51	41.99	42.74

Table 2: Results for Tamil and Telugu

the true frequent morph length range.

- However for Telugu, morph length parameter did not improve the results at the most frequent morph length range (5-8).
- *Concentration parameter* (α) too influences the effect of base distribution as a whole, but at present, our study does not take into account α. For small α values, the base distribution will not have much effect.

7 Conclusion

In this paper, we mainly studied the effect of knowledge of morph length that could have on the accuracy of morphological segmentation of agglutinative languages. Towards that goal, we introduced a simple unsupervised morphological segmentation model based on Bayesian approach that utilized prior distribution over morph length. The results showed that the knowledge of length certainly has a positive impact on the accuracy. Also, the model provided competitive results in general and achieved best overall performance (F-score: 48.83%) for Tamil against Morfessor. As a future work, it would be interesting to see the model and priors that handle *sandhi* changes.

Acknowledgements

The research leading to these results has received funding from the European Commission's 7th Framework Program (FP7) under grant agreement n° 238405 (CLARA). We would like to thank David Mareček for useful suggestions about theory and implementation of the system. We also would like to thank anonymous reviewers for their useful comments.

References

Akshar Bharathi, Rajeev Sangal, Dipti M Sharma and Radhika Mamidi. 2004. Generic Morphological Analysis Shell. *In Proceedings of LREC 2004.*

Benjamin Snyder and Regina Barzilay. 2008. Unsupervised Multilingual Learning for Morphological Segmentation. In *Proceedings of the 46th Annual Meeting of the Association for Computational Linguistics (ACL)*, pages 737–745. 2008.

David Yarowsky and Richard Wicentowski. Minimally Supervised Morphological Analysis by Multimodal Alignment. In *Proceedings of the 38th Annual Meeting on Association for Computational Linguistics (ACL)*, 2000.

Dhanalakshmi V, AnandKumar M, Rekha RU and Rajendran S. 2009. Morphological Analyzer for Agglutinative Languages Using Machine Learning Approaches. In *Advances in Recent Technologies in Communication and Computing*, 2009, ARTCom'09, 2009.

Hoifung Poon, Colin Cherry and Kristina Toutanova. 2009. Unsupervised Morphological Segmentation with Log-Linear Models. In *Proceedings of Human Language Technologies: The 2009 Annual Conference of the North American Chapter of the ACL (NAACL-HLT)*, pages 209–217, Boulder, Colorado, June 2009.

Jason Naradowsky and Sharon Goldwater. 2009. Improving Morphology Induction by Learning Spelling Rules. In *Proceedings of 21st International Joint Conference on Artificial Intelligence (IJCAI)*, 2009.

Jason Naradowsky and Kristina Toutanova. 2011. Unsupervised Bilingual Morpheme Segmentation and Alignment with Context-rich Hidden Semi-Markov Models. In *Proceedings of the 49th Annual Meeting of the Association for Computational Linguistics: Human Language Technologies*, pages 895–904, June, 2011.

John Goldsmith. 2001. Unsupervised Learning of the Morphology of a Natural Language. *Computational Linguistics*, 27(2): pages 153–198, 2001.

Kimmo Koskenniemi. 1983. Two-level morphology: A general computational model for word-form recognition and production. Publication 11, University of Helsinki, Department of General Linguistics, Helsinki. 1983.

Madhavi Ganapathiraju and Lori Levin. 2006. TelMore: Morphological Generator for Telugu Nouns and Verbs. *In Proceedings of the Second International Conference on Digital Libraries*. 2006.

Mathias Creutz. 2003. Unsupervised Segmentation of Words Using Prior Distributions of Morph Length and Frequency. In *Proceedings of the 41st Annual Meeting of the Association for Computational Linguistics (ACL)*, pages 280–287, July 2003.

Mathias Creutz and Krista Lagus. 2005. Unsupervised Morpheme Segmentation and Morphology Induction from Text Corpora Using Morfessor 1.0. In *Publications in Computer and Information Science*, Report A81, Helsinki University of Technology, 2005.

Mathias Creutz and Krister Lindén. 2004. Morpheme Segmentation Gold Standards for Finnish and English. Publications in Computer and Information Science, Report A77, Helsinki University of Technology, October, 2004.

Matthew G. Snover and Michael R. Brent. 2001. A Bayesian model for morpheme and paradigm identification. In *Proceedings of the 39th Annual Meeting on Association for Computational Linguistics (ACL)*, pages 490–498, 2001.

Sai Kiranmai G., K. Mallika, M. Anand Kumar, V. Dhanalakshmi and K. P. Soman. 2010. Morphological Analyzer for Telugu using support vector machines. *In Proceedings of ICT 2010.*

Sajib Dasgupta and Vincent Ng. 2007. High-Performance, Language-Independent Morphological Segmentation. In *Proceedings of NAACL HLT 2007*, pages 155–163, 2007.

Sharon Goldwater, Thomas L. Griffiths and Mark Johnson. 2006. Contextual dependencies in unsupervised word segmentation. In *In Proceedings of the 21st International Conference on Computational Linguistics and 44th Annual Meeting of the Association for Computational Linguistics (ACL)*, 2006.

Sharon Goldwater, Thomas L. Griffiths and Mark Johnson. 2009. A Bayesian framework for word segmentation: Exploring the effects of context. *Cognition*, 112 (1), pp. 21–54, 2009.

Uma Maheshwar Rao G., Amba Kulkarni P. and Christopher Mala. 2011. A Telugu Morphological Analyzer. *International Telugu Internet Conference Proceedings, Milpitas, California, USA, 28th - 30th September, 2011*

Vera Demberg. 2007. A Language-Independent Unsupervised Model for Morphological Segmentation. In *Proceedings of the 45th Annual Meeting of the Association of Computational Linguistics (ACL)*, pages 920–927, Prague, Czech Republic, June 2007.

Walter R. Gilks, Sylvia Richardson and David Spiegelhalter. 1996. Markov Chain Monte Carlo in Practice. Chapman and Hall. 1996.

Xiao Z., McEnery A., Baker P. and Hardie A. 2004. Developing Asian language corpora: standards and practice. In *Proceedings of the Fourth Workshop on Asian Language Resources*, pp. 1–8, 2004.

Young-Suk Lee. 2004. Morphological Analysis for Statistical Machine Translation. In Proceedings of the HLT-NAACL 2004, pp. 57–60, Boston, USA, 2004.

A Comparable Corpus Based on Aligned Multilingual Ontologies

Roger Granada
PUCRS (Brazil)
roger.granada@acad.pucrs.br

Lucelene Lopes
PUCRS (Brazil)
lucelene.lopes@pucrs.br

Carlos Ramisch
University of Grenoble (France)
ceramisch@inf.ufrgs.br

Cassia Trojahn
University of Grenoble (France)
cassia.trojahn@inria.fr

Renata Vieira
PUCRS (Brazil)
renata.vieira@pucrs.br

Aline Villavicencio
UFRGS (Brazil)
alinev@gmail.com

Abstract

In this paper we present a methodology for building comparable corpus, using multilingual ontologies of a scpecific domain. This resource can be exploited to foster research on multilingual corpus-based ontology learning, population and matching. The building resource process is exemplified by the construction of annotated comparable corpora in English, Portuguese, and French. The corpora, from the conference organization domain, are built using the multilingual ontology concept labels as seeds for crawling relevant documents from the web through a search engine. Using ontologies allows a better coverage of the domain. The main goal of this paper is to describe the design methodology followed by the creation of the corpora. We present a preliminary evaluation and discuss their characteristics and potential applications.

1 Introduction

Ontological resources provide a symbolic model of the concepts of a scientific, technical or general domain (e.g. Chemistry, automotive industry, academic conferences), and of how these concepts are related to one another. However, ontology creation is labour intensive and error prone, and its maintenance is crucial for ensuring the accuracy and utility of a given resource. In multilingual contexts, it is hard to keep the coherence among ontologies described in different languages and to align them accurately. These difficulties motivate the use of semi-automatic approaches for cross-lingual ontology enrichment and population, along with intensive reuse and interoperability between ontologies. For that, it is crucial to have domain-specific corpora available, or the means of automatically gathering them.

Therefore, this paper describes an ontology-based approach for the generation of multilingual comparable corpora. We use a set of multilingual domain-dependent ontologies, which cover different aspects of the conference domain. These ontologies provide the seeds for building the domain specific corpora from the web. Using high-level background knowledge expressed in concepts and relations, which are represented as natural language descriptions in the labels of the ontologies, allow focused web crawling with a semantic and contextual coverage of the domain. This approach makes web crawling more precise, which is crucial when exploiting the web as a huge corpus.

Our motivation is the need of such resources in tasks related to semi-automatic ontology creation and maintenance in multilingual domains. We exemplify our methodology focusing on the construction of three corpora, one in English, one in Portuguese, and one in French. This effort is done in the context of a larger research project which aims at investigating methods for the construction of lexical resources, integrating multilingual lexica and ontologies, focusing on collaborative and automatic techniques (http://cameleon.imag.fr/xwiki/bin/view/Main/).

In the next section, we present some relevant related work (§2). This is followed by a description of the methodology used to build the corpora (§3). Finally, the application example expressed by the resulting corpora are evaluated (§4) and discussed

(§5). We conclude by outlining their future applications (§ 6).

2 Related Work

Web as corpus (WAC) approaches have been successfully adopted in many cases where data sparseness plays a major limiting role, either in specific linguistic constructions and words in a language (e.g. compounds and multiword expressions), or for less resourced languages in general[1].

For instance, Grefenstette (1999) uses WAC for machine translation of compounds from French into English, Keller et al. (2002) for adjective-noun, noun-noun and verb-object bigram discovery, and Kim and Nakov (2011) for compound interpretation. Although a corpus derived from the web may contain noise, the sheer size of data available should compensate for that. Baroni and Ueyama (2006) discuss in details the process of corpus construction from web pages for both generic and domain-specific corpora. In particular, they focus on the cleaning process applied to filter the crawled web pages. Much of the methodology applied in our work is similar to their proposed approach (see §3).

Moreover, when access to parallel corpora is limited, comparable corpora can minimize data sparseness, as discussed by Skadina et al. (2010). They create bilingual comparable corpora for a variety of languages, including under-resourced ones, with 1 million words per language. This is used as basis for the definition of metrics for comparability of texts. Forsyth and Sharoff (2011) compile comparable corpora for terminological lexicon construction. An initial verification of monolingual comparability is done by partitioning the crawled collection into groups. Those are further extended through the identification of representative archetypal texts to be used as seeds for finding documents of the same type.

Comparable corpora is a very active research subject, being in the core of several European projects (e.g. TTC[2], Accurat[3]). Nonetheless, to date most of the research on comparable corpora seems to focus on lexicographic tasks (Forsyth and Sharoff, 2011; Sharoff, 2006), bilingual lexicon extraction (Morin and Prochasson, 2011), and more generally on machine translation and related applications (Ion et al., 2011). Likewise, there is much to be gained from the potential mutual benefits of comparable corpora and ontology-related tasks.

Regarding multilingually aligned ontologies, very few data sets have been made available for use in the research community. Examples include the vlcr[4] and the mldirectory[5] datasets. The former contains a reduced set of alignments between the thesaurus of the Netherlands Institute for Sound and Vision and two other resources, English WordNet and DBpedia. The latter consists of a set of alignments between web site directories in English and in Japanese. However, these data sets provide subsets of bilingual alignments and are not fully publicly available. The MultiFarm dataset[6], a multilingual version of the OntoFarm dataset (Šváb et al., 2005), has been designed in order to overcome the lack of multilingual aligned ontologies. MultiFarm is composed of a set of seven ontologies that cover the different aspects of the domain of organizing scientific conferences. We have used this dataset as the basis for generating our corpora.

3 Methodology

The main contribution of this paper is the proposal of the methodology to build corpora. This section describes the proposed methodology presenting our own corpus crawler, but also its application to construct three corpora, in English, Portuguese, and French. These corpora are constructed from the MultiFarm dataset.

3.1 Tools and Resources

Instead of using an off-the-shelf web corpus tool such as BootCaT (Baroni and Bernardini, 2004), we implemented our own corpus crawler. This allowed us to have more control on query and corpus construction process. Even though our corpus construc-

[1] Kilgarriff (2007) warns about the dangers of statistics heavily based on a search engine. However, since we use the downloaded texts of web pages instead of search engine count estimators, this does not affect the results obtained in this work.

[2] `www.ttc-project.eu`

[3] `www.accurat-project.eu`

[4] `www.cs.vu.nl/~laurah/oaei/2009`

[5] `oaei.ontologymatching.org/2008/mldirectory`

[6] `web.informatik.uni-mannheim.de/multifarm`

tion strategy is similar to the one implemented in BootCaT, there are some significant practical issues to take into account, such as:

- The predominance of multiword keywords;
- The use of the fixed keyword *conference*;
- The expert tuning of the cleaning process;
- The use of a long term support search AP[b].

Besides, BootCaT uses the Bing search API, which will no longer work in 2012. As our work is part of a long-term project, we preferred to use Google's search API as part of the University Research Program.

The set of seed domain concepts comes from the MultiFarm dataset. Seven ontologies from the OntoFarm project (Table 1), together with the alignments between them, have been translated from English into eight languages (Chinese, Czech, Dutch, French, German, Portuguese, Russian, and Spanish). As shown in Table 1, the ontologies differ in numbers of classes, properties, and in their logical expressivity. Overall, the ontologies have a high variance with respect to structure and size and they were based upon three types of resources:

- actual conferences and their web pages (type 'web'),
- actual software tools for conference organisation support (type 'tool'), and
- experience of people with personal participation in organisation of actual conferences (type 'insider').

Name	Type	C	DP	OP
Ekaw	insider	74	0	33
Sofsem	insider	60	18	46
Sigkdd	web	49	11	17
Iasted	web	140	3	38
ConfTool	tool	38	23	13
Cmt	tool	36	10	49
Edas	tool	104	20	30

Table 1: Ontologies from the OntoFarm dataset in terms of number of classes (C), datatype properties (DP) and object properties (OP).

Currently, our comparable corpus generation approach focuses on a subset of languages, namely English (`en`), Portuguese (`pt`) and French (`fr`). The labels of the ontology concepts, like *conference* and *call for papers*, are used to generate queries and retrieve the pages in our corpus. In the current implementation, the structure and relational properties of the ontologies were ignored. Concept labels were our choice of seed keywords since we intended to have comparable, heterogeneous and multilingual domain resources. This means that we need a corpus *and* an ontology referring to the same set of terms or concepts. We want to ensure that the concept labels are present in the corresponding natural language, textual sources. This combination of resources is essential for our goals, which involve problems such as ontology learning and enriching from corpus. Thus, the original ontology can serve as a reference for automatically extracted resources. Moreover, we intend to use the corpus as an additional resource for ontology (multilingual) matching, and again the presence of the labels in the corpus is of great relevance.

3.2 Crawling and Preprocessing

In each language, a concept label that occurs in two or more ontologies provides a seed keyword for query construction. This results in 49 `en` keywords, 54 `pt` keywords and 43 `fr` keywords. Because many of our keywords are formed by more than one word (average length of keywords is respectively 1.42, 1.81 and 1.91 words), we combine three keywords regardless of their sizes to form a query. The first keyword is static, and corresponds to the word *conference* in each language. The query set is thus formed by permuting keywords two by two and concatenating the static keyword to them (e.g. *conference reviewer program committee*). This results in $1 \times 48 \times 47 = 2,256$ `en` queries, 2,756 `pt` queries and 1,892 `fr` queries. Average query length is 3.83 words for `en`, 4.62 words for `pt` and 4.91 words for `fr`. This methodology is in line with the work of Sharoff (2006), who suggests to build queries by combining 4 keywords and downloading the top 10 URLs returned for each query.

The top 10 results returned by Google's search

API[7] are downloaded and cleaned. Duplicate URLs are automatically removed. We did not filter out URLs coming from social networks or Wikipedia pages because they are not frequent in the corpus. Results in formats other than html pages (like .doc and .pdf documents) are ignored. The first cleaning step is the extraction of raw text from the html pages. In some cases, the page must be discarded for containing malformed html which our page cleaner is not able to parse. In the future, we intend to improve the robustness of the HTML parser.

3.3 Filtering and Linguistic Annotation

After being downloaded and converted to raw text, each page undergoes a two-step processing. In the first step, markup characters as interpunctuation, quotation marks, etc. are removed leaving only letters, numbers and punctuation. Further heuristics are applied to remove very short sentences (less than 3 words), email addresses, URLs and dates, since the main purpose of the corpus is related to concept, instance and relations extraction. Finally, heuristics to filter out page menus and footnotes are included, leaving only the text of the body of the page. The raw version of the text still contains those expressions in case they are needed for other purposes.

In the second step, the text undergoes linguistic annotation, where sentences are automatically lemmatized, POS tagged and parsed. Three well-known parsers were employed: Stanford parser (Klein and Manning, 2003) for texts in English, PALAVRAS (Bick, 2000) for texts in Portuguese, and Berkeley parser (Petrov et al., 2006) for texts in French.

4 Evaluation

The characteristics of the resulting corpora are summarized in tables 2 and 3. Column D of table 2 shows that the number of documents retrieved is much higher in `en` than in `pt` and `fr`, and this is not proportional to the number of queries (Q). Indeed, if we look in table 3 at the average ratio of documents retrieved per query (D/Q), the `en` queries return much more documents than queries in other languages. This indicates that the search engine returns more distinct results in `en` and more duplicate URLs in `fr` and in `pt`. The high discrepancy in

[7] research.google.com/university/search

	Q	D	W token	W type
en	2,256	10,127	15,852,650	459,501
pt	2,756	5,342	12,876,344	405,623
fr	1,892	5,154	9,482,156	362,548

Table 2: Raw corpus dimensions: number of queries (Q), documents (D), and words (W).

	D/Q	S/D	W/S	TTR
en	4.49	110.59	14.15	2.90%
pt	1.94	120.08	20.07	3.15%
fr	2.72	115.63	15.91	3.82%

Table 3: Raw corpus statistics: average documents per query (D/Q), sentences per document (S/D), words per sentence (W/S) and type-token ration (TTR).

the number of documents has a direct impact in the size of the corpus in each language. However, this is counterbalanced by the average longer documents (S/D) and longer sentences (W/S) in `pt` and `fr` with respect to `en`. The raw corpus contains from 9.48 million words in `fr`, 12.88 million words in `pt` to 15.85 million words in `en`, constituting a large resource for research on ontology-related tasks.

A preliminary semi-automated analysis of the corpus quality was made by extracting the top-100 most frequent n-grams and unigrams for each language. Using the parsed corpora, the extraction of the top-100 most frequent n-grams for each language focused on the most frequent noun phrases composed by at least two words. The lists with the top-100 most frequent unigrams was generated by extracting the most frequent nouns contained in the parsed corpus for each language. Four annotators manually judged the semantic adherence of these lists to the conference domain.

We are aware that semantic adherence is a vague notion, and not a straightforward binary classification problem. However, such a vague notion was considered useful at this point of the research, which is ongoing work, to give us an initial indication of the quality of the resulting corpus. Examples of what we consider adherent terms are *appel á communication (call for papers)*, *conference program* and *texto completo (complete text)*, examples

	# of adherent terms	
	Lower	Upper
en words	46	85
en n-grams	57	94
fr words	21	69
fr n-grams	24	45
pt words	32	70
pt n-grams	11	45

Table 4: Number of words and n-grams judged as semantically adherent to the domain.

of nonadherent terms extracted from the corpus were *produits chimiques (chemical products), following case, projeto de lei (law project).* In the three languages, the annotation of terms included misparsed and mistagged words (*ad hoc*), places and dates typical of the genre (but not necessarily of the domain), general-purpose terms frequent in conference websites (*email, website*) and person names.

Table 4 shows the results of the annotation. The lower bound considers an n-gram as semantically adherent if all the judges agree on it. The upper bound, on the other hand, considers as relevant n-grams all those for which at least one of the four judges rated it as relevant. As a result of our analysis, we found indications that the English corpus was more adherent, followed by French and Portuguese. This can be explained by the fact that the amount of internet content is larger for English, and that the number of international conferences is higher than national conferences adopting Portuguese and French as their official languages. We considered the adherence of Portuguese and French corpora rather low. There are indications that material related to political meetings, law and public institutions was also retrieved on the basis of the seed terms.

The next step in our evaluation is verifying its comparable nature, by counting the proportion of translatable words. Thus, we will use existing bilingual dictionaries and measure the rank correlation of equivalent words in each language pair.

5 Discussion

The first version of the corpus containing the totality of the raw pages, the tools used to process them, and a sample of 1,000 annotated texts for each language are freely available for download at the CAMELEON project website[8]. For the raw files, each page is represented by an URL, a language code, a title, a snippet and the text of the page segmented into paragraphs, as in the original HTML file. A companion log file contains information about the download dates and queries used to retrieve each URL. The processed files contain the filtered and parsed texts. The annotation format varies for each language according to the parser used. The final version of this resource will be available with the totality of pages parsed.

Since the texts were extracted from web pages, there is room for improvement concerning some important issues in effective corpus cleaning. Some of these issues were dealt with as described in the § 3, but other issues are still open and are good candidates for future refinements. Examples already foreseen are the removal of foreign words, special characters, and usual web page expressions like "site under construction", "follow us on twitter", and "click here to download". However, the relevance of some of these issues depends on the target application. For some domains, foreign expressions may be genuine part of the vocabulary (e.g. *parking* or *weekend* in colloquial French and *deadline* in Portuguese), and as such, should be kept, while for other domains these expressions may need to be removed, since they do not really belong to the domain. Therefore, the decision of whether to implement these filters or not, and to deal with truly multilingual texts, depends on the target application.

Another aspect that was not taken into account in this preliminary version is related to the use of the relations between concepts in the ontologies to guide the construction of the queries. Exploiting the contextual and semantic information expressed in these relations may have an impact in the set of retrieved documents and will be exploited in future versions of the corpus.

6 Conclusions and Future Work

This paper has described an ontology-based approach for the generation of a multilingual compara-

[8] `cameleon.imag.fr/xwiki/bin/view/Main/Resources`

ble corpus in English, Portuguese and French. The corpus constructed and discussed here is an important resource for ontology learning research, freely available to the research community. The work on term extraction that we are doing for the initial assessment of the corpus is indeed the initial step towards more ambitious research goals such as multilingual ontology learning and matching in the context of our long-term research project.

The initial ontologies (originally built by hand) and resulting corpora can serve as a reference, a research resource, for information extraction tasks related to ontology learning (term extraction, concept formation, instantiation, etc). The resource also allows the investigation of ontology enriching techniques, due to dynamic and open-ended nature of language, by which relevant terms found in the corpus may not be part of the original ontology. We can also assess the frequencies (relevance) of the labels of the ontology element with respect to the corpus, thus assessing the quality of the ontology itself. Another research that can be developed on the basis of our resource is to evaluate the usefulness of a corpus in the improvement of existing multilingual ontology matching techniques[9].

Regarding to our own crawler implementation, we plan to work on its evaluation by using other web crawlers, as BootCaT, and compare both approaches, specially on what concerns the use of ontologies.

From the point of view of NLP, several techniques can be compared showing the impact of adopting different tools in terms of depth of analysis, from POS tagging to parsing. This is also an important resource for comparable corpora research, which can be exploited for other tasks such as natural language translation and ontology-based translation. So far this corpus contains English, Portuguese and French versions, but the ontology data set includes 8 languages, to which this corpus may be extended in the future.

[9] An advantage of this resource is that the Multilingual OntoFarm is to be included in the OAEI (Ontology Alignment Evaluation Initiative) evaluation campaign.

References

Marco Baroni and Silvia Bernardini. 2004. BootcaT: Bootstrapping corpora and terms from the web. In *Proc. of the Fourth LREC (LREC 2004)*, Lisbon, Portugal, May. ELRA.

Marco Baroni and Motoko Ueyama. 2006. Building general- and special-purpose corpora by web crawling. In *Proceedings of the 13th NIJL International Symposium on Language Corpora: Their Compilation and Application*, pages 31–40.

Eckhard Bick. 2000. *The parsing system Palavras*. Aarhus University Press.

Richard Forsyth and Serge Sharoff. 2011. From crawled collections to comparable corpora: an approach based on automatic archetype identification. In *Proc. of Corpus Linguistics Conference*, Birmingham, UK.

Gregory Grefenstette. 1999. The World Wide Web as a resource for example-based machine translation tasks. In *Proc. of the Twenty-First Translating and the Computer*, London, UK, Nov. ASLIB.

Radu Ion, Alexandru Ceauşu, and Elena Irimia. 2011. An expectation maximization algorithm for textual unit alignment. In Zweigenbaum et al. (Zweigenbaum et al., 2011), pages 128–135.

Frank Keller, Maria Lapata, and Olga Ourioupina. 2002. Using the Web to overcome data sparseness. In Jan Hajič and Yuji Matsumoto, editors, *Proc. of the 2002 EMNLP (EMNLP 2002)*, pages 230–237, Philadelphia, PA, USA, Jul. ACL.

Adam Kilgarriff. 2007. Googleology is bad science. *Comp. Ling.*, 33(1):147–151.

Su Nam Kim and Preslav Nakov. 2011. Large-scale noun compound interpretation using bootstrapping and the web as a corpus. In *Proc. of the 2011 EMNLP (EMNLP 2011)*, pages 648–658, Edinburgh, Scotland, UK, Jul. ACL.

Dan Klein and Christopher D. Manning. 2003. Accurate unlexicalized parsing. In *Proc. of the 41st ACL (ACL 2003)*, pages 423–430, Sapporo, Japan, Jul. ACL.

Emmanuel Morin and Emmanuel Prochasson. 2011. Bilingual lexicon extraction from comparable corpora enhanced with parallel corpora. In Zweigenbaum et al. (Zweigenbaum et al., 2011), pages 27–34.

Slav Petrov, Leon Barrett, Romain Thibaux, and Dan Klein. 2006. Learning accurate, compact, and interpretable tree annotation. In *Proc. of the 21st COLING and 44th ACL (COLING/ACL 2006)*, pages 433–440, Sidney, Australia, Jul. ACL.

Serge Sharoff, 2006. *Creating general-purpose corpora using automated search engine queries*. Gedit, Bologna, Italy.

Inguna Skadina, Ahmed Aker, Voula Giouli, Dan Tufiş, Robert Gaizauskas, Madara Mieirina, and Nikos Mastropavlos. 2010. A Collection of Comparable Corpora for Under-resourced Languages. In Inguna Skadina and Andrejs Vasiljevs, editors, *Frontiers in Artificial Intelligence and Applications*, volume 219, pages 161–168, Riga, Latvia, Oct. IOS Press.

Ondřej Šváb, Vojtěch Svátek, Petr Berka, Dušan Rak, and Petr Tomášek. 2005. Ontofarm: Towards an experimental collection of parallel ontologies. In *Poster Track of ISWC 2005*.

Pierre Zweigenbaum, Reinhard Rapp, and Serge Sharoff, editors. 2011. *Proc.of the 4th Workshop on Building and Using Comparable Corpora: Comparable Corpora and the Web (BUCC 2011)*, Portland, OR, USA, Jun. ACL.

Author Index